SMALL HOURS OF THE NIGHT

Selected Poems of ROQUE DALTON

Edited by Hardie St. Martin

Translated by
Jonathan Cohen, James Graham,
Ralph Nelson, Paul Pines,
Hardie St. Martin and David Unger

Curbstone Press

FIRST EDITION, 1996
Copyright © 1996 by Aida Cañas
Translation Copyright © 1996 by the respective translators
All Rights Reserved

Printed in the U.S. on acid-free paper by Bookcrafters
Cover design: Naomi Taubleb

Curbstone Press is a 501(c)(3) nonprofit publishing house whose
programs are supported in part by private donations and by
grants from: ADCO Foundation, Witter Bynner Foundation for
Poetry, Connecticut Commission on the Arts, Connecticut Arts
Endowment Fund, The Ford Foundation, The Greater Hartford
Arts Council, Junior League of Hartford, Lawson Valentine
Foundation, LEF Foundation, Lila Wallace-Reader's Digest
Literary Publishers Marketing Development Program
administered by CLMP, The Andrew W. Mellon Foundation,
National Endowment for the Arts, Puffin Foundation, and
United Way-Windham Region.

Library of Congress Cataloging-in-Publication Data

Dalton, Roque. 1935-
    Small hours of the night : selected poems of Roque Dalton /
edited by Hardie St. Martin : translations by Jonathan
Cohen ... [et al.].
        p.   cm.
    ISBN 1-880684-35-7
    1. St. Martin, Hardie. II. Cohen, Jonathan. III. Title.
PQ7539.2.D3A6   1996
861—dc20   96-867

published by
CURBSTONE PRESS   321 Jackson Street   Willimantic, CT 06226
phone: (860) 423-5110   e-mail: curbston@connix.com
WWW at http://www.connix.com/~curbston/

I'm especially grateful to Jon Cohen for his invaluable cooperation on the two long poems we translated together, to David Unger for his helpful comments and suggestions, to Jim Graham, who did more than his share and came up with excellent solutions, and to Robert Irwin and Sandy Taylor for their encouragement and patience with my neverending changes and revisions.

Hardie St. Martin

Earlier versions of Hardie St. Martin's translations appeared in the following publications: *Nimrod, Street Magazine, Quarry West, Lumen/Avenue A, The Nation, Practices of the Wind,* and *Machete.*

Earlier versions of James Granham's translations appeared in *Machete, Cover,* and *Contact II.*

Some of these translations have appeared in *American Poetry Review* and *Compost.*

TRANSLATORS

[JC] Jonathan Cohen
[JG] James Graham
[RN] Ralph Nelson
[PP] Paul Pines
[DU] David Unger
[HSM] Hardie St. Martin

CONTENTS

TAVERN AND OTHER PLACES

SMALL HOURS OF THE NIGHT

I Remember Roque Dalton

I remember a laughing Roque Dalton. Skinny, pale, his bones sticking out, big-nosed like me, and always laughing. I don't know why I always remember you laughing, Roque Dalton. A laughing revolutionary. Not that revolutionaries are particularly serious, not at all, but he was a revolutionary that laughed all the time. First of all he laughed at himself. He laughed at silly little things about El Salvador and was forever talking about it, because he really loved his "Tom Thumb" country. Naturally he laughed at the Salvadoran bourgeoisie and would make us all laugh. He would laugh at the Jesuits with whom he had studied and in whose school he had "lost his faith" (he would also laugh at this expression) to join the Communist Party, and he'd also laugh at things about the Party. (Still it was his Party.) He would tell fantastic stories about El Salvador that seemed to be made up but were actually true. A man was in jail—a real sewer—, covered with cockroaches, for several years. He was crazy when they let him out and he didn't mind roaches the least bit; he would smile blissfully and, for him, being covered with roaches was like being covered with butterflies. Roque Dalton was in prison once, they were going to shoot him. What's more, they were going to make the Party believe he was a CIA informer and spy to make sure he wouldn't be considered a martyr. He didn't believe in God, but he prayed that night, he knelt down in his cell and prayed. As "mad luck" would have it, he said, there was an earthquake that night; the prison's walls collapsed and he escaped. Cintio Vitier and Fina and I laughed at him, telling him that what he called "mad luck" we called something else, and he also laughed. Roque was always in a great humor despite the horrible things he had been through, and the horrible things still waiting ahead that he had a premonition about. Roque Dalton's commitment to the Revolution was like a marriage contract. He was married to the Revolution. It was his destiny not only to sing it but also to give his life for the Revolution. Now he is reembodied in many lives, he has come back to life in El Salvador's insurrection. He's always laughing, in spite of the massacres, in spite of the weeping. He is laughing because he feels victorious. As if he were already the victor. Roque Dalton will soon be children's parks, schools, hospitals; he will be the poems he wrote and many others not written yet. Roque Dalton will be a laughing, happy population of Roque Daltons.

—Ernesto Cardenal
1980

From *Recopilación de textos sobre Roque Dalton*, Editorial Casa de las Americas, Havana, 1986.

ROQUE DALTON
Poet and Revolutionary

A scarce twenty years after his tragic, senseless death, the complex facts of Roque Dalton's life have been overlaid—or in many cases clarified and defined—by myth. Even among his closest friends it is nearly impossible to talk about Roque without falling into verbal chiaroscuro effects: superlative and anecdotal exaggerations. His prolific artistic production, cut off at the age of forty, remains a monumental artifact: testimony to his tortuous journey through the twentieth century, revealing his contradictory, dialectical, love-hate relationship with the country of his birth—El Salvador—both in and out of exile, and illustrating his profound conviction that the poet can and must, in his life as well as in his work, serve as the finely-honed scalpel of change, both in word and deed, when he lives in a profoundly unjust, stagnant society.

First, let's take the myth surrounding the undeniable fact of his birth in San Salvador in the year 1935. His father, one of the members of the outlaw Dalton brothers, after a career of robbing banks, disappeared from Kansas and settled in El Salvador with his ill-gotten fortune. He invested it in coffee plantations and grew even richer without any interference from the law.

He left Roque his surname and a Jesuit education.

Roque's mother was a registered nurse whose salary supported the family decorously, but Roque learned about class differences at an early age—in fact, during his first day of kindergarten at Santa Teresita del Niño Jesús, and I quote:

> ...where I took
> my first steps in society
> smelling faintly of horse shit:
> "Peasant!" Roberto called me
> that first day of class
> in the kindergarten section,
> and he gave me a hard shove ...

His illegitimate birth and his status as outcast in a rich kid's school nurtured his resentment, and they were undoubtedly determining causes for the defiant posture Roque was to assume from adolescence on. He was the smartest in his class and was chosen as valedictorian on graduation day. He took advantage of the occasion to deliver a blistering attack on the hypocrisy of his Jesuit instructors who slavishly supported the prejudices of the rich majority at the school and tolerated, if they didn't actively encourage, the students' wretched discrimination against their Christian brothers who happened to have been born poor, or out of wedlock.

After a year at the University of Santiago, Chile, Roque returned to the University of San Salvador in 1956, where he helped found the University Literary Circle just before the Salvadoran military set fire to the school building. The following year, Roque traveled to the Moscow Youth Festival and on his return joined the Communist Party. He was arrested in 1959 and again in October 1960, the charges against him on this latter occasion reading in part: "He has formed red cells among workers, students and peasants, especially inciting these last to protest and to employ violence against the landowners . . ."

Once again myth intervenes. Roque was not tried or sentenced in any civil court, but—according to legend—he was sentenced to be executed by firing squad. The day before the sentence was to be carried out—on 26 October 1960—dictator Colonel José María Lemus was overthrown by a coup d'état and Roque's life was saved. He spent the year 1961 in Mexican exile, writing much of his early poetry: *The Window in My Face* and *The Injured Party's Turn*. He dedicated the latter book to the Salvadoran police chief who had filed charges against him: "To General Manuel Alemán Manzanares, who by securing my severe punishment paid me the greatest compliment of my life, although to tell the truth it was a bit exaggerated."

Roque, reflecting on this phase of his life, later wrote:

"My actual writings were so insignificant that they weren't even mentioned in the police charges: General Manzanares acted to rectify a real vacuum in my life. I took a solemn oath that, from then on, I myself would undertake to provide the proofs against me to the judge. For this reason I chose my actual profession."

The ambiguity of the last sentence is revealing. Did Roque consider poetry to be a profession? Naturally! It was a consuming passion that he cultivated with professional intensity. But in the previous sentence he speaks about providing "the proofs against me to the judge," and clearly, given the context, he was not referring to the judge of a poetry contest. Obviously, when he wrote that dedication, Roque considered himself a professional revolutionary. And—of course—a poet.

Roque achieved a seamless union between those two callings. His personal ethics and aesthetics, forged in the incandescent reality of El Salvador, produced a human being whose personal life and poetry were of a single piece. His gift for self-mockery saved him from ever falling into the sanctimonious pose that frequently accompanies revolutionary fervor. That he was perfectly aware of the gesture he had made of his life is evident in one of his last epigrammatic poems, "Poetic Art" (1974):

> Poetry
> forgive me for helping you understand
> that you're not made of words alone.

Roque was already a militant revolutionary when the Cuban revolution (January 1959) produced seismic aftershocks in the social conscience of all Latin Americans. It must have been an extraordinary experience for a twenty-four-year-old poet to see his revolutionary convictions vindicated, and even more so for Roque, who, because he not only voiced his convictions but acted in accord with them, had already been sentenced to death for the first time.

After putting an end to his Mexican exile in December 1961, Roque naturally gravitated to Havana, Cuba, where he received a warm welcome from the Cuban and Latin American exiled writers who gathered in the Casa de las Américas. Revolutionary Cuba offered young Latin American poets the unusual opportunity to publish their works, and Roque took full advantage of it. His first book, *Mine with the Birds,* was published in El Salvador in 1958, and his second, The *Window in My Face* appeared in Mexico in 1961. From then on, starting with *The Injured Party's Turn* and *The Sea* in 1962, almost all of his poetic work as well as much of his prose, was published in Cuba.

But Roque not only wrote poetry and literary essays during that first period in Cuba; he also received military training to prepare for his return to El Salvador. It should be remembered that this was during the tumultuous post-revolutionary period when not only Fidel Castro and Che Guevara but many other Central American and Caribbean revolutionaries were confident that the Cuban revolution was destined to trigger a series of emulative upheavals (with a little help from Fidel) throughout the area. Roque returned clandestinely to El Salvador in the summer of 1965 to continue his bittersweet love affair with his small homeland and to resume the political work that had been interrupted by his imprisonment and exile.

Clandestinity back in those days wasn't taken very seriously and a short two months after his arrival, destiny intervened to keep the Roque legend growing. One day Roque was bored and, with the poet Italo López Vallecillos, he went to Niña Concha's bar where the best *conchas negras* and the coldest beer in San Salvador was to be had. He was still licking the foam off his upper lip when two plainclothes police walked in and arrested him. He was held incommunicado, tortured, interrogated and threatened by the CIA, and once again sentenced to death.

Roque awaited execution in Cojutepeque Prison when destiny, this time in the form of the 1965 earthquake, stepped in once more to add to his legendary dossier. The quake shattered the outer wall of his cell and Roque was able to dig his way out through the rubble of stones and mortar and escape with shaky legs and a few scratches. He slipped into a religious procession that had been passing in front of the prison when the earthquake hit—another minor miracle—and his fellow conspirators smuggled him out of El Salvador. He returned to Cuba and a few months later the Party sent him to Prague as correspondent for The International Review: Problems of Peace and Socialism.

Roque and I never coincided in time or space; nevertheless, we corresponded frequently over the years, and we had a number of friends in common. It was Roque who initiated the interchange during his time in Prague from 1965 to 1967. I was living in Paris in

those days, and we both shared the same nostalgia for our distant—
and in Roque's case, forbidden—homeland. The strange thing about
his letters was that they only touched peripherally on politics and
poetry. Instead, they were filled with comical accounts of daily life
in Prague, and above all they dealt with Salvadoran cooking. For
months we exchanged recipes for dishes that were almost impossible
to prepare in Europe, and especially in Prague, for lack of the right
ingredients. How could one duplicate the mysterious alchemy of *gallo
en chicha*, for example, or recreate the subtle aroma of *pupusas de
loroco*?

He passed through Paris once when I wasn't there and asked
about me when he went to visit Julio Cortázar. Aurora, Julio's first
wife, told me later:

"He has a strange, disquieting expression: I feel he's going to meet
a tragic death."

"No way," I told her, "Roque has more lives than a cat."

Some years later we nearly crossed paths in Cuba. It was in 1968
and I had been invited by the Casa de las Américas to serve as a judge
in its poetry contest. My plane was delayed for three days for lack of
repair parts ("La Cubana llega cuando le da la gana") and mutual
friends told me Roque had come to the airport three consecutive days
with bunches of flowers to welcome me. When I finally got there he
had been sent to a remote part of the island on a mysterious mission.
During the next weeks he bombarded me with a series of little folded
papers—messages he had scribbled in free moments and had sent
with friends who were returning to Havana. These were almost always
delivered to me at lunch time in the dining room. I remember that
one of them said: "We really blew it, Claribel. Here I am, the son of a
gringo, and you're married to another."

Years later in Mexico, long after Roque's death, Eraclio Zepeda,
one of his great drinking buddies, swore to me that Roque had
assured him that I danced the rumba and the samba incomparably
well and that I had taught him to dance the samba. This marvelously
Daltonian fable inspired me to write a poem.

On the international scene the 1960's was a period of reflux for
Latin American revolutionaries. From Prague, Roque contemplated
the failure of guerrilla movements in Guatemala, Nicaragua,

Colombia and Peru and heard of the death of Che Guevara in Bolivia. The foquista theory that sprang from the success of the Cuban revolution was totally discredited by this chain of disasters, and Latin leftists composed self-criticisms and engaged in bitter, divisive debates about a new point of departure for the revolution in each country. During this period Roque never wavered in his conviction that the revolution in El Salvador could only come about through armed struggle. This view separated him from the Salvadoran Communist Party that maintained an official line of "legalism" and "accumulation of strength." Neither the "objective" nor the "subjective" conditions for a popular uprising existed in El Salvador at that time, and Roque decided to throw in his lot with a small group of Guatemalan revolutionaries that later to became the nucleus of the Guerrilla Army of the Poor (EGP). His mysterious absence when I visited Cuba in 1968 was due to a second period of military training.

His book, *Tavern and Other Places*, reflecting his long stay in Prague, won the Casa de las Américas poetry prize in 1969 and established Roque, at age thirty-four, as one of the best young poets in Latin America. The EGP guerrilla movement did not mature until 1972, so Roque joined the staff of Casa de las Américas and spent the next five years working there, at the Prensa Latina news agency and for Radio Havana, while continuing to publish other books of poetry and an occasional monograph.

By the early 1970's the revolutionary spirit started gaining momentum in El Salvador, and Roque sought admission to the clandestine ranks of the Fuerzas Populares de Liberación (FPL). Its leader, Comandante Marcial, turned him down, saying that his place in the revolutionary ranks was as a Marxist poet and writer rather than as a foot soldier.

Anyone familiar with Roque's impassioned militancy and with his long-standing conviction that a revolutionary poet could not remain on the sidelines but had to take an active part in the struggle, could have guessed that he would not follow that advice. And he didn't. Instead, he made contact with another guerrilla organization, the Ejército Revolucionario del Pueblo (ERP) which accepted his offer of enlistment.

Another prerequisite for his transition from intellectual and poet to clandestine warrior was submission to plastic surgery. His aquiline nose, flapping ears and long, thin face were too familiar to Salvadorans for him to pass unrecognized. After all, he had only survived two months in hiding in 1965 before being picked up. He emerged from the clinic with his ears tucked back, a thick mustache, spectacles with tortoise shell frames, another hairdo and a higher forehead: the perfect example of a serious young business executive.

Roque entered El Salvador in disguise and with false documentation at the end of 1973. He disappeared into the underworld of airtight secrecy. During the next eighteen months he wrote *Clandestine Poems*.

As a person, Roque radiated an exuberant vitality that illuminated each of the manifold aspects of his life: his poetry, his pitiless sense of self-ridicule, his revolutionary will, his inextinguishable curiosity, his need to know and explain the complex, contradictory world in which he moved.

One of the consequences of this vitality was his prolific output: eighteen volumes of poetry and prose before his premature death at age forty. Another was his apparent impatience about revising and reworking his poems. Despite the fact that many of his epigrams are as polished and hard-edged as diamonds, one has the impression that they were not mulled over and patiently honed, but that they simply came into his head, and he jotted them down, probably on the back of an envelope or perhaps on a bar napkin and stuffed them in his shirt pocket. Rereading his work, one cannot avoid the sensation (clarified, no doubt, by ex-post-facto knowledge of what was to come) that he was a writer in a hurry; that he somehow knew his time was measured, his days counted, and that he had to take advantage of each moment, whatever the activity in which he was engaged.

One of the constants in his work was his continual advance in the dominion of form, his progress toward an ever more direct use of language and his tenacious dialogue with the Muse of Poetry, whom he consulted, scolded and flattered until finally, in *Tavern*, he exploded:

Ah, poetry of today:
with you it is possible to say everything.

By the time he wrote *Clandestine Poems* he had gained the self-confidence of a triumphant lover who had wooed and won his twin muses: Poetry and Revolutionary Struggle.

Despite the great confidence with which he managed his poetic instrument and the revolutionary optimism with which he viewed the future, things were not going well within his own organization, the ERP. Roque insisted on the need to forge links with the incipient mass organizations that held promise of becoming a powerful political factor in the country. A military faction, on the other hand, with a short-range coup d'état strategy, accused him of treacherously trying to divide the organization. It was this group that condemned him to death, executing him on 10 May 1975, four days before his fortieth birthday.

Ironically enough, this monstrous act did precipitate the division of the ERP, The Resistencia Nacional (RN) split off to create still another politico-military organization. And not only that, Roque's policy of forging links between the clandestine politico-military organizations and the open mass organizations came to be the accepted line for all the principal revolutionary movements.

Roque's senseless death closed the circle of myth and legend that had surrounded him from the beginning. For Latin American revolutionaries, Roque was converted into a martyr, and his literary reputation grew as his posthumous work was published.

It was Roberto Armijo who telephoned me from Paris—we were then living in Mallorca—to give me the shocking news of Roque's death, stammering out confused versions of how it happened, since at first nobody knew the truth.

That same evening, as I was trying with all my might to comprehend the incomprehensible and to accept this irreparable loss, which in some measure we all felt, I told my husband that I felt like reading him some of Roque's poems in order to feel a bit closer to Roque. I took down *The Injured Party's Turn* from the shelf, opened it at random and the first verse my eyes focused on was this:

When you know that I have died, don't say my name...

As the tears sprang to my eyes and stopped my voice, I thought: Yes, Roque, you rascal, of course that's you: the immaterial materialist sending me from beyond the grave another of your little papers.

—Claribel Alegría

LOVE FALLS LIKE A GENEROUS RAIN

... I've been saying for a while now that the major poet of today must have, to build a body of work, two necessary starting points: profound understanding of life, and his or her own imaginative liberty ... Out of this experience, gained through years of hard, wonderful everyday comings and goings, the imagination, with its expressive instruments (style, artistic genre), will be able to undertake the making of the great work of art if the proprietor of that imagination has a clear conception of creative freedom and of his or her responsibilities regarding beauty.

Roque Dalton
"Poetry and Militancy in Latin America"

After Roque's graduation from the exclusive Externado de San José private school, run by the Jesuits, his father Winnall Dalton sent him to study law in Chile, where he entered the non-denominational National University in Santiago. Its liberal atmosphere, his friendship with Leftist students, some lectures by Mexican painter Diego Rivera gradually sharpened his interest in Socialism and his thinking took a radical turn. Reading Marx, he explained years later, had made him see his country in the true light: a place where people were dying of hunger, misery, illnesses, and exploitation.

Homesick for El Salvador after eleven months in Chile, he came back a changed person. He enrolled in law school at the University of El Salvador where, a year later in 1955, together with a young exiled Guatemalan poet, Otto René Castillo[1], he founded El Círculo Literario Universitario (The University Literary Circle) which brought together the country's best young writers, poets many of them. They joined forces with those students whose "subversive" unrest had started to make El Salvador's military government feel threatened and were among the first to speak out openly against the repressive forces then in power. In 1956 the military set fire to the University and in 1959 Roque was thrown into prison for the first time. In 1960 the military bore down on the students in the University, with the usual methods and instruments of a police state. There were brutal beatings and arrests. The poet was put behind bars once again. Sometime before the first of these last two events he joined the Communist Party.

Looking back at those years, in one of several interviews[2] conducted in Havana he explained, "Suddenly I saw that I had an urgent need to say many things about my country, about man, about what was on my mind. And the instrument I found at hand . . . the one that seemed to me just and correct, was the word written in a beautiful way— that's what I understand poetry is—and since then, today, what I expect to go on being until I die is a revolutionary poet truly conscious of the problems of his time . . . ."

Roque Dalton felt that he had been a victim of a misdirected education and this haunted him all his life. He revisited his childhood in many poems; some are irreverent, even aggressive, yet carry echoes of the Bible as well as prayers and hymns from the liturgy of the Catholic Church. In *La ventana en el rostro* (*The Window In My Face*) we find his first bitter words for the Jesuits who, in school, had prescribed: "humility penitence / is enough for now . . . for that soul of yours as tiny / as a sparrow's little asshole." They had had his future all lined up for him: Law or perhaps Medical School, a good state job, a new Chevrolet and of course membership in the Country Club where he could get drunk and "vomit if you like / next to the Minister's first cousin"; but he "must absolutely stay out of politics (except under the guidance of the Professor of Religion . . .)." Roque Dalton can be a lovable clown—often pointing his humor playfully at himself—but his irony can be venomous.

Love and death—constant references in all his future work— weave in and out of the poems in this book. The poet finds much in common between the two: there's an inner reality in him, where they constantly meet, sometimes with high tension. "Love is one of death's faces," he said, and it's a defense mechanism as well, a shield against the death outside, the one he suspected all his life was always around the corner. And on a different level, the erotic love the poet so often falls back upon provides a means of withdrawal into his private emotional life, away from the hostile external reality threatening him.

In one of his last books there's a love poem in which he could still say, "in (your nakedness) I was able to find sanctuary from the police."

In the Havana interview Roque Dalton remarked that "Henri Michaux opened [for him] the field of the imagination, of pure creativity." With the use of the Belgian poet's "imaginative, imagining attitude, an attitude of the imagination constantly in ebullition . . . extraordinary results might be obtained" as long as—he throws this in for safet measure—the good Socialist poet didn't lift his feet completely off the ground.

In the poems of the first section of *El turno del ofendido* (*The Injured Party's Turn*)[3] Roque Dalton trusted his creative imagination for the words and images needed to communicate a complex spiritual experience that wouldn't fit comfortably in prescribed form. Systematically hounded, harassed, imprisoned, tortured, and sentenced to face a firing squad, after a narrow last minute escape, he was finally forced into exile. In the first poems of this book a spirit of terrible loss and defeat prevails: ". . . once again you can call me poor brother shattered comrade wretch / grateful like a dog for his nightly bread" ("The Decision"). Two magnificent long poems, "La noche" ("The Night") and "Las cicatrices" ("The Scars"), give a touching likeness of the poet caught up in spiritual crisis, wrestling with his soul over unsettled differences between the present he has chosen and the past he has rejected. In the first of these poems, he's alone in his hotel room, "gravely wounded by life," forgotten by everyone, when the night comes to him like a protective mother and lover at the same time. But he becomes suspicious and accuses her of laughing at him; he calls her a poisoned bitch and sends her off to put on her clothes in someone else's room, to find another corpse to lean on and leave him alone to wipe off her long trail of blood. Imaginary voices come in through the walls to mock him: "apostate, fugitive, runaway husband, wicked son, convicted militant, childish idiot, grotesque angel, confused and trembling there." At last, he remembers that daylight—a symbol for the life outside—brings no respite, only hatred and suffering, so he turns again for comfort to the dark, where it's "incomparably beautiful / to fall to stay to be reborn in the night / . . . to copulate with it as if it were a welcome swamp / and take it in like something that will be tattooed on my heart." The scenes in the six sections of this poem (I've included only IV, "The Disciple," in my selection) follow one another in quick irrational order. This is perhaps the first example of a procedure borrowed from the movies, "montage, the succession of uninterrupted images," that Roque Dalton admitted was of singular importance to his work.

In "The Scars" the narrator attacks the frivolity and vices of the rich, the greed of the Church, and the inhumanity of his persecutors, "those little yellow men with the face of a treacherous dog ... right down to its last gold fang." Hunted down, he has been running all his life. At last, when a shadow stands in his way, he stops with relief, "Here's a friendly hand an answer / to hide in ... God." Only to find that God has turned against him and all the while has actually been at the bottom of his troubles. In the end he is proud that he has come through, has been able to soak his wounds in fresh clay and has even had time to let his nails grow out and to prepare his first stone. From now on the initiative would be his, and he would strike back.

In a less personal section of this book, subtitled "Through the Keyhole," the poet is no longer the center of interest, he looks at society with a colder eye. This part contains a series of wonderful cameo poems, brief but effective sketches of persons—including satirical pieces on "Christ," "theologians," "the Church," "The Pope,"—and incidents seen or heard from the perspective of that indiscreet hole. Had he written nothing else, some of the poems in this book alone would, I believe, have earned our lasting respect for him.

Surreal imagery, which had made a timid appearance in his first book, is a strong element in *El mar* (*The Sea*), yet nowhere that I know of does Roque Dalton even mention the word "surrealism." Was it perhaps because César Vallejo, the poet he most admired, had discredited it in his essay "Autopsy on Surrealism"? *The Sea* consists of a single poem, rightfully standing alone because it is in a category by itself, unrelated to anything else Roque Dalton ever wrote. In it, as the poet's mind wanders back over old voyages to ports of call in Latin America and Europe, the lilting lines seem to join the rhythm of the sea. Half-drunk and sleepy, the poet brings his audience back home to a beach where, the moment and the sea having become blurred, he decides to have one last drink of his bad rum, go on back up the beach and head for his bed.

In a copy of *Los testimonios* (*The Testimonies*) preserved in the Casa de las Americas in Havana there is a marginal note in Roque Dalton's own handwriting that reads: "This book is actually an accumulation of material that, had it been fully developed, would have filled four books . . . ." In effect, The Testimonies seems to have been put together arbitrarily. In the first part the poet recreates or reinvents some of the Indian myths he had discovered while studying anthropology at the Universidad Autónoma de México, where he had enrolled shortly after going into exile. Stripped of what the Spanish poet Antonio Machado called its cosmetics, and largely free of the rhetoric that in his earlier books had betrayed a weakness for Neruda's grand manner, his poetry takes on a plainer surface, going from complex to simple statement. The conversational tone—a reflection of César Vallejo's influence—of his previous work persists but the language is strictly colloquial. Part way through this book the poet slips into prose; with no clear division between poetry and prose, many of the pieces in this section are clearly on the side of poetry, but others seem to be casual observations, too flat to be called poems. Much of this book seems to be an experimental stopover on the poet's way to his later major poetry.

In 1970 *Los pequeños infiernos* (*Minor Hells*) was brought out by Ochos, a poetry series published by Libres de Sinera in Barcelona. A small selection of remarkable lyric poems, it is obviously not the book the poet had originally had in mind. Some of its poems had appeared in *The Injured Party's Turn* and *Taverna y otros lugares* (*Tavern and Other Places*), both of which had been published before in Cuba.

By the time he wrote *Tavern and Other Places*, his most ambitious and successful book of poetry, Roque Dalton had full control over his material and the technical devices he had been preparing all along. It's divided into three sections. The first is aptly named "El país" (I, II, III) ("The Country" I, II, III), which is the section's central theme; it reflects the poet's tragic vision of El Salvador's past and his dedication to its troubled present, with so many of his countrymen dead that they were becoming a restless majority. The poems in Part I pinpoint or flash unsparing light on crucial moments in the history of this country and its record of long repression under a string of rulers whose systematic abuse of power has taken place with the blessing or indifference of a handful of wealthy landowners. Part II is a dramatic sketch of the country seen from a distorted angle by six members of an aristocratic English family that had known better days in England and has moved to El Salvador with the hope of getting rich again. Failing to adjust, they restrict themselves to their own small circle—letting in only a local bishop who shares their views—and react with contempt and disgust toward a people they consider inferior. They are shown up as typical foreigners or colonists who are ultimately defeated by a Third World culture they can't understand and therefore detest.

Subtitled "Poems from the Last Prison," the first section of Part III is an almost day-to-day record—his thoughts, feelings, humiliation and loneliness—of the poet's life in prison, "a sad mudhole of mourning." The final poem of this group is a soliloquy in which the speaker feels death measuring, ripening, separating him from a familiar world, and begins to hallucinate:

> herido estoy viene la muerte

> (I'm badly hurt and death is on its way)

He accepts all the suffering thrown at him for upholding the truth and is willing to pay for it with his life. The poem ends on a suspended note, with this unfinished phrase

> pero por la verdad
> la muerte
> pero por la verdad

> (but for the sake of the truth
> death
> but for the sake of the truth)

The "Six Prose Poems" of the second section interrupt the book's formal structure. Admirable as they are, these independent pieces are simply a change of pace; they allow the poet to touch on a variety of themes ranging from an enigmatic tragi-comic piece expressing love-hate-love for his country to a satirical attack on the dogmatic misuse of the word by writers of social realism. The first prose poem starts off on a satirical note: "From the Spanish Conquest on, my country has been laughing like an idiot through a gaping wound. It's almost always nighttime here and that's why you can't see it bleed." And in the last piece—apparently a kind of apologia for his own later work—he raps Pablo Neruda's knuckles for sometimes being a kind of zombie in the poetry he wrote after *Residencia en la tierra*, overloading it with useless words; then he charges Stalin with trying to turn words into "exceptions of dialectical materialism" and eventually bringing about their degeneration into lifeless Soviet prose. But between those pieces there are two exceptional prose poems: the moving account of the first time Roque Dalton met his father and another called "El té," an ironic portrait, sad and hilarious at the same time, of six illiterate jailed criminals whose only pastime is a few games of poker at "tea time" in their cell: a pathetic scene that slowly unfolds like an elegant English ritual with all the trimmings— fine silver spoons, exquisite porcelain, and Flemish linen—served by an Indian with only one arm, the other having been hacked off with a machete by his own brother years before.

Written between 1966 and 1967, while the poet was on the editorial board of the *International Review* (*Problems of Peace and Socialism*) in Prague, where he lived for two years, "Tavern" is, in the author's own words, "virtually a chronicle of the mental schemes of an important sector of Czech youth." It's an assemblage of conversations overheard in U Fleku, a tavern in Prague popular with European and Latin American students and young intellectuals. The poem was almost prophetic of the upheaval that would shake Czechoslovakia in the spring of 1968 and be brutally squashed by the Russian Army. Apart from calling on all the resources in verse and prose that he had been holding in reserve, the poet exploits typography to obtain a variety of compelling effects: the changes in type provide a clue to the shifts in the dialogue from one speaker to the next, suggest variations in the volume or tone of each person's voice and sometimes even mark the pace of the conversations. There's a strength in the poems of *Tavern and Other Places* that comes from years of work finding the right form to go with the things the poet wanted to say. His use of montage is particularly effective in the title poem-collage.

A persistent note of humor holds together the poems in *Un libro levemente odioso* (*A Slightly Repellent Book*) and the laughter so many people seem to remember him for is almost audible in them. And yet Roque Dalton was never more serious. Anyone or anything can be the target of his wry, irreverent humor, his devastating wit. There are no exceptions. His country, its President, the Army, society, politics, Christianity (with parodied lines from the Ave María and the Lord's Prayer), poets, and even the writer himself. The black humor running through many of these poems is passed off under the semblance of playful verse; however, most of them are short but destructive as knife thrusts. Here are samples:

To a man whose death means nothing to the people at his funeral he says:

> Everyone is happy: from now on
> you were going to be the earth's problem,
> long seed in the basement of the grass.

To a general:

> Just go ahead and wash yourself
> there in that pool of blood.

And to the poet:

> Life pays its bill with your blood
> and you go on believing you're a nightingale.

Finally there's a poem, "Polemics," about the decrepit nature of politics in Latin America:

> Young Theodore Petkoff says
> that the accusation of "Trotskyist"
> served as a condom
> to avoid the conception and birth

of new ideas in the heart
of the Latin American
Communist movement.

I disagree.

What good is a condom
in an old men's home?

In the selection offered here there are poems from two books that
have not yet been published: *El Amor me cae más mal que la pimavera*
(*Love Hits Me Harder Than Springtime*) and *Los hongos* (*Toadstools*).
The poems I've included were taken from the best and most complete
anthology[4] I've seen of Roque Dalton's poetry. I don't know what final
form the first book will take but, in the composite interview already
referred to, the poet said: "I'm working on a long poem, 'Toadstools,'
that in a way focuses on the struggle that existed, when I was young,
between my revolutionary conscience and my Christian conscience,
solved (in a somewhat Joycean style) in a Jesuit school. It's intended
to be a long letter to my professor of philosophy in that school." The
book is made up of a twelve-part poem dedicated to Ernesto
Cardenal. It's amazing how throughout his work Roque Dalton kept
coming back to the subject of the God of his childhood, the non-
existent enemy he apparently was never able to forgive or keep
completely out of his mind.

No selections from *Las histories prohibidas del Pulgarcito* (*The
Banned Histories of Tom Thumb*) are included here, because that book
has been well represented in *Poems*, translated by Richard Schaaf and
brought out by Curbstone Press. And I haven't used anything from
Poemas clandestinos, which was published complete in English by
Solidarity Publications, San Francisco.

✳ ✳ ✳

Roque Dalton's poetry was written in prison, in exile, in moments
of loneliness and silent anger, in hiding or on the run from death.
Most of his admirers fondle a romantic memory of the tireless

revolutionary, the martyr, ignoring how much he loved poetry for itself. He was always conscious of being a poet. In spite of its lapses, his is the solid work of one of the best and most representative poets of his time. In November of 1967 he said, "I've been writing at quite a fast pace: for some years now I've always had to make myself write in haste, as if I knew they were going to kill me the next day."

He might have saved his life by tying himself to a comfortable desk like so many other theorists and activists in his Party, but he was not just talking when he said

> Politics are taken up at the risk of life
> or else you don't talk about it.

and

> Learning to die,
> that's what life was.

—Hardie St. Martin

THE WINDOW IN MY FACE

STUDY WITH A LITTLE TEDIUM

Clov: He's crying.
Hamm: Then he's living.
Endgame *by Beckett*

Fifteen years old and I cry every night.

I know there's nothing special about this,
that there are better things in this world
to tell you about in my singing voice.

Even so I drank wine for the first time today
and stayed in my room naked, so I could take in the afternoon
carved into small pieces
by the clock.

Thinking alone hurts. There's no one to hit, no one
to pardon and mercifully let off the hook.
Only you and your face. You and your face
of a phony saint.

The scar no one has ever seen comes into view,
the grimace we hide every day,
the face I've never been able to bury, it will make us cry and
                                    break down completely
on the day the good people know everything
and even the birds deny us love and a song.

Fifteen years of being tired
and I cry every night just to make believe I'm alive.

Maybe none of you understands what I'm talking about.

It's my first wine talking not me
while the skin weighing me down swallows the shade.
[JG]

THE CRAZY ONES

Names have never sat well with us crazy ones.

All the others
wear their names like a new suit of clothes,
when they make new friends they babble their names,
they're in a rush to print them on tiny white cards
that pass from hand to hand,
filled with the joy of innocent things.

And what happiness they radiate, those Alfredos and Antonios,
those hard-luck Juans and silent Sergios,
those Alejandros rank with the musk of the sea!

All those names flowing out of the same throat
that calls them out like proud flags on a battlefield,
names still kicking around on earth making noise
even after they've gone off with their bones into the shadows.

But the crazy ones, O Lord, the crazies
who suffocate from forgetting so much,
we poor crazy cats get even our laughter mixed up
and our happiness fills with tears,
how are we going to get anywhere dragging our names along,
looking out for them,
polishing them like miniature silver animals,
seeing with these eyes that even dreams can't control,
that don't get lost in the dust that flatters and hates us?

We mad ones just can't hope to have anyone name us
but we'll forget about this too...
[JG]

TIME FOR ASHES

September draws to a close. It's time to tell you
how hard it has been not to die.

This afternoon, for instance,
in my gray hands I hold
beautiful books I don't understand,
I can't sing even if the rain has stopped
and the memory of the first dog I loved
as a boy hits me out of the blue.

From the time you left yesterday
even the music is damp and cold.

When I die,
they'll remember only my obvious joy each morning,
my flag that hasn't the right to collapse,
the hard facts I passed around at the fireside,
the fist I made unanimous
with the stone cry hope demanded.

It's cold without you. When I die,
when I die
they'll say, meaning well,
that I didn't know how to shed tears.

It's raining again now.
It has never been so late at a quarter to seven
as it is today.

I have this wild itch to laugh
or kill myself.
[HSM]

HATING LOVE

I don't believe in angels
but the moon is now dead for me.
The last glass of wine is gone
before the thirst I'm suffering from.
The blue grass lost its way
running away from your sails.

The butterfly setting her color
on fire was made of ashes.
The morning fires off
dewdrops and silent birds.
I feel ashamed of being naked
and as vulnerable as a child.

Without your hands my heart
is the enemy in my chest.
[HSM]

MONDAY

Six o'clock in the morning
screaming its way out of the clock: once more
the cathedral of light will bring its wall down
on my itinerant heart
resting just now.

I hate giving up the bed covers as much as I hate any bourgeois.

It's not because of the cold, there isn't any.
Not that I'm afraid of the eye lurking
where the street lamp
crucified the darkness
last night.
It's not even because of you
or your sex exploding in my hands,
your exposed grotto
dying a minute ago in the water.

It's
—oh hesitation
a shattered blue year had coming to it—
just that feeling as old as my left fist
or my longed-for understanding of birds:
the eye close to my shoulder, never even pleading,
the hand near my face I lift like a new stone,
life asking me for
the little energy I admit in myself.

What I say is I should have come
—not into the world of puppets, silk sewing baskets,
coarse bottles of gin that are like hospitals for thirst,
not into the world you offer me or the one I offer you,
fragile bread, field
for the butter knife—

I should have come, let me say it again,
like a naked fire
to the dry forest where I'm terrified without crying out,
like a rush of water that's hard on the helpless sand,
like a tree that asks the sleeping earth for blood,
a complaint of pregnancy against evasion,
against the tear that never comes
and overpowering despair...

But early on
I came just as I am,
with hands that can bleed,
with fear,
with love,
with four Mondays to each month.
And I believe
that if it weren't for this heart,
this throbbing musical planet,
by now I'd have gone off to try and die.
In spite of everything,
I wouldn't want to forget how to laugh...
[HSM]

MY HORSE

I owned a horse
more beautiful and nimble than the light.

Stamping, he was like a wave of blood.
A tiny storm with eyes.
An untamed mountain on perfectly molded legs.

My horse was born dead one day
and the shock on my face put the winds to flight...
[HSM]

LISTEN

The first thing you have to do is shout,
throwing all that bad stuff into the air ...

Listen, all of you,
those of you who receive my word like a blessing to ward off the
night.
Listen, listen
even during a future outrage when they'll give you a bloody
head and smashed-up legs
breaking your horizon between the stones that never sold out
or gave a machete a rough swing
against water or footsteps.
Listen,
you over there,
those I insulted with the most obvious truth,
those I gave handouts with arrogance,
those I loved with my flags and my fingernails,
those I wounded with my rambling love,
those of whom I knew only
their secret code,
their share of my air and my enemy.
Listen,
women,
girls I almost deflowered with this voice I had to steal,
sweet figures with which they painted heaven for me,
lovers,
rivers of meat someone dammed up in order to slake my thirst,
eyes that hemmed in the night I asked for,
little noses, hands with fingers kept away from the fire,
lips, armpits like the black roses
that hid before asking if anyone wanted them,
feet of a ballerina
where my expatriate heart ended up dying.
Listen,
listen,

hard friends who scorned the tenderness
of my unending childhood,
sons, grandfathers of alcohol and transitive dawns,
evil builders
of the desperation traveling inside of watches;
knives I shied away from,
grapes, milk and honey I'd hoped to obtain
like someone who kisses the sugar's soul,
pirates ransacking the tears of the fugitives,
crazy ones, crazy and dear, lovers of flowers and vices,
of the eyes of their child who was never born,
of the small velvet bear whose ears they wanted to kiss;
proud enemies I wanted to love;
mother,
mother who was a shout away from my impetuous shipwrecks,
mother, my mother mother,
the one beautiful shadow
capable of hating every inch of him who rightly
shut the window in my face;
listen,
listen,
hear my final shout,
the unrestrained accent of my hardest rivers,
the vibrant banner
mine alone and closest to my heart...
[JG]

POEMS-IN-LAW TO LISA

> *Let's go! Let's go! I'm wounded...*
> —César Vallejo

I

Lisa:
from the moment I started loving you
I've hated my Professor of Civil Law.

How can I concentrate on Supply and Demand
that look to me like the windows of a jail,
on the Theory of Motives that makes me think of a tunnel
full of red crickets and frustrated roots that never see the sun,
on mortgages sick with TB,
on the registry
of aggressive real estate?
Can I think about all this, I mean,
if right in front of my anguish I have your enormous eyes
                                        as uncomplicated
and dark as a pond late at night,
your voice as fresh as tomorrow's dawn,
—ah, my fugitive—whose musical fragrance
I save on the fingers of my right hand?
Lisa, transparent
daughter of the air:
the morning sun in the meadow asks me for
your nakedness,
my hands going down from the flower of the water
to save your blood
from the green arteries of the grass.

And I, poor slave of this century,
an unfinished servant of boredom and blood,
I'm writing you, loving you, while everyone discusses
One Party Non-Negotiated Arrangements.

Ah, Lisa, Lisa, I'm
completely broken up.

II

Poor guy, my dearest,
here alone with my terror among the Legal Codes,
here with my law books, poor jail bait
denying heaven among fat guys
who actually believe in rhinoceroses,
always thinking that we'll find a bar
where if we throw out the tables
there'll be enough room for the dawn and you in front of my eyes.
Poor me,
poor fool,
a Marxist and I'm eating my nails:
I love the soft hooks in the sand,
the words of the sea and the innocence of the gulls;
I detest the Banks,
B-complex injections,
the nighttime cruelty of the motorcyclists
hurling their heavy bricks at the angel of dreams,
I'm in bad shape, my love,
me a poor kid who never carved his name on a tree,
of whom everyone these days is demanding
that he read Jellinek with a smile
and get into bed naked with Customs and Tariffs,
and swear before the wind that the judge is superior to the assassin.

Ah Lisa, Lisa,
I'm a terrible wreck.
[JG, HSM]

DREAM FAR AWAY FROM TIME

There was a time
when I knew a lot about the dead.

Whenever I stopped to face the night
in the last streets my sorrow
could bear,
I would make out their voices clearly,
hailing me through my country's mist
and reminding me over and over
that some day I'd have to throw in my lot
with the infinite ice of bodies that were lost.

I knew how the dead whirled around
shaking their terrifying crystal manes,
wearing the ivy's battle dress,
eager to use their sacred animal selves
they had saved up from this life.

God was someone dead I couldn't understand.

Learning how to die,
that's what life was.

Now
after new hymns, new oceans of tears,
after new eyes present behind the numbers,
from steady, cruel, never-ending bonfires,
from silent houses
where husbands love their naked brides,
from the dead body in the hospital
solid friend unmoved by my question,
from winters that bleed ahead of time,
from churches that grow on and on

over the initials of the slave, I
know
  that
    the
      dead
        raised
          their
            flag
and left us, miserable sons of oblivion,
to the life we still have to build,
country, sea or cosmic life,
cleansed of the old obstacles
(of darkness or special silences)
and of its solemn images
and secret outcries
hidden in the trees.

The dead are dead.
They've stayed behind.
Dead.
[HSM]

VERNACULAR ELEGY FOR FRANCISCO SORTO

*Francisco Sorto is a common criminal in El Salvador's
Central Penitentiary who's gone crazy on account of four
years of incarceration in wretched cell No. 9. Crazy as he is,
he strolls silently among the prisoners and in the afternoons,
when he sees the swallows and the parakeets from the prison
patio, he sings—with watery eyes and a voice bereft of
rhythm—old songs of Carlos Gardel's...*

For nine years Francisco Sorto
has been a prisoner.

He killed because he had to kill
because he had to be terrible and hard
in his barren countryside where no one ever speaks of bread
in his countryside parched parched parched
where the dust falls solitary upon blind laughter
and the illiterate brain
shouts its burned music and its boundless weeping.

Francisco Sorto has
nine eyes of confinement.

Nine shouts for light where the centuries dance
like little children.

Nine "nineteen hundred and so many" frights.

Nine years scratching his lice-infested heart,
nine years of scaring himself
with a curse on the tip of his teeth.

Nine black tears of silence and of cold.

Nine tall lieutenants
who make us weep
laughing after they fire their pistols into the air,

talking about rivers, fresh timber on the banks,
of fields that don't even have a stone wall
where you can sleep with your belly to the stars.

Nine years, dammit,
nine years disguised as blows to the head
while you're tied up;
nine years, nine,
nine years that can't be crammed into the mouth of the world,
nine years of which it could be said
that they are only seventy-eight thousand
eight hundred and forty hours
if you knew anything about school desks and figures.

Beautiful Francisco Sorto
with his monkey face
clean
like the damp earth that hears the sound of our feet.
Francisco Sorto all alone
in the middle of eight hundred prisoners.
Francisco Sorto without visitors on Sundays.
Francisco Sorto curing his wounds
with the excrement of hens.
Francisco Sorto four years in darkness
handcuffed, four very hard years in solitary.
Francisco Sorto,
how great
and marvelous, how great a man you are,
that even now you haven't forgotten how to sing!
[JG]

MINOR CHORUS OF THE FIFTH CELL

*(It's getting darker. They still haven't taken
the guitars down from the walls.
A cup of coffee, a cigarette.)*

Once again they've closed the cell door.
It's closed...closed.
Closed, closed, closed.

Will we get out this month?
Ah, that's what you call luck!
A month,
a month between your hand and hope!

I who have to wait a spell
of fourteen years, what else can I tell you,
I who am going to leave when I'm fifty,
I remember nothing about rivers anymore,
I who can't remember to remember anything,
I who don't even know any songs, nor want to,
I who wouldn't even know how to walk in the street,
I who am serving five years on my second offense,
I who because of that pale-faced fat juror now stand here whistling,
fist on my jaw and heart on my back,
I who because the D.A. never saw my mother
blind the poor woman from crying for me and I innocent
nearly without blame
for the necessities of his vulture's career,
I on account of poverty eternal and complete,
I on account of being an idiot, a good man,
I because I had to teach the world a lesson,
I because I said it was so,
I because I spit my refusal in the dust,
I because I spit,
I because
I 'cause
I

and the door
and the closed door
and the door of the cell is closed,
closed, closed, closed,
closed,
closed...
[JG]

THE INJURED PARTY'S TURN

THE DECISION

(Juárez and Balderas, 9:30 P.M.)

And though the heart may not be the spirited creature we had hoped
it will do to passionately take in love and the knives all around us.
The whole immense city sees itself a prisoner on this corner
that's like an enormous eye
opening to where infinity begs an end to man's thirst for going too far.

I've already recovered my flashing sign:
I deny ecstasy and exalt the bitter serenities
with a tight smile and an old clean suit I swear I'll accept all
the deaths I have coming
but not those of the women with watery eyes I left sunk deep in silence
their hands—salty with tears—touching their souls that I'd
trampled with my elegant hooves.

Everything was decided long seconds ago—ah my reckless
adventure falls down in life so stubbornly—
so that warm friendships are no longer necessary,
season of tenderness in this twelve-hour nocturnal year.

Just the same—my desires betray me!—my smile escapes
towards those sweet efforts like a young green dove and once again
you can call me poor brother shattered comrade wretch
grateful like a dog for his nightly bread.

Ah, but what of death: hurl—what does it matter—the deepest lures
even throw life over afterwards, if you want, like an avalanche
to accept is to be and I accepted it all
everything
even the one word you don't want to say for fear of a deadly
complicity in its obstinate warmth.
[JG]

20

ISLAND ON THE FIFTH FLOOR

It's not the heat, no.
I've had no alcohol that can explain this fever.
From my window I see people passing
like curious spiders lost in the smoke.

The smoke.
Out of the tall chimneys it wraps itself around everything.

If it weren't for the smoke I might go out to look for a woman,
a glass of water, something
still living off the world's diminishing freshness.

My childhood
also remained on the other side of the smoke.
[JG]

STORM

A tremendous wind is blowing.
It's only a small hole in my chest
But a tremendous wind is blowing through it...
Henri Michaux

I
(10:00 p.m.)

Another glassful of dust
from the earth's ashes
let a lamp come up from the belly of the sea
a teardrop for my throat today
another echo quenching its thirst
in my blood because it has to

Let's kneel and shed tears for the hidden dead
let's seek justice for those everyone passes up

Outside the rain shakes out its dull draperies
the cold is black grass growing over the sidewalks

II
(11:30)

One day I felt cold but no one noticed me.

Only my tiniest pore was alert.

The ice wanted to tell me something.
Tender words, I'm sure. It didn't have time to.

The heat's greedy arms to the rescue!
How sickening—rats, god, mother, how sickening!

And from then on, the ice has been my enemy...

III
(1:00 a.m.)

Deep hair
hands like spiders in search of its deepness
I'll stay here away from the rain
with my last solitary drink.

When the day ends
—each of these days—
loneliness tries to take over even my shadow.

I can hear an angel's cough
an angel's baby cough.

Someone has lighted the candles they had forgotten all about.
[HSM]

STILLBORN PARABLE

The beetle who loves to quarry dung
and work on filth like a goldsmith
doesn't want to put up with the mint.

Nor will any of you accept my truth.

And you don't even know your refusal strangles your eyes
and cuts off all the air
you had coming.

It's okay. Everyone will join the fighting in his own way.
As for those who are naked, that's their business!
[HSM]

THE BAD EXAMPLE

They made me choose between selling out and the wall
and it was a wall of knives.

And since I couldn't help getting cut up
son of the worst plague they said to me
he doesn't love his blood
refuses to keep it in
and unties the knots of his veins.

Outraged all the mothers in the city wouldn't weep
that day not even for the slit throats of the onions.

I hope at least the little children will come unto me.
[HSM]

BECAUSE I SPOKE OUT

The last hired mourner went off
to look for comfort among fools.

(I could stand naked in this huge town square
lit up by the phosphorescences of the stillness
and there would be no intruders to stare at me.

Oh this desertion is deadly
it makes its own chill sprout from the flames.)

I hope someone will come to hear me again
and weep with me to the end.

Maybe then I'll be strong enough to make the truth less bitter.
[HSM]

I SEE

I think they've lied to us enough.

Now I have the key to the hieroglyph
pain gave me between fits of a drunk's laughter
lungers from a jailer and glares from a rabid dog
without a heart.

This much I also know: it will be difficult to make men accept
this nakedness someone who possesses the light reverts to
hard to convince them that so far all the laughs were turned against
                                                                    them
and that all the hands held out to them had cruel nails.

(It's a little chilly but it's better that way
now that the mortal fires
the flushed faces in the middle of the orgy
the feverish myth invented by the wine settled in your blood
and spider webs clinging to the tongue have all disappeared.)

I'm going to strip some of the last veils off right now.

And I'll be the one
to take care of the wounds.
[HSM]

INSOMNIA

The sky is a huge lake the lake
is a small sky

(In this sanitarium you can even hear the stones scream
the pines like long fingers sticking out of the grave
receive solid shadows from the moon
smoky black or granite shadows

I'd like to return to El Salvador
but I don't know if it's a country dreamed of
nothing but wishful thinking
born of the green fire of my illness.)

Insomnia is a red or violet net
a bottomless well
not even daybreak can see the end of
a flaming crucifix
that never burns out

Was that a bell far off
or my heart?

Once again it's four
in the morning.
[HSM]

THE DISCIPLE

from *La Noche*

Hieronymus Bosch must have been the only sane man
in the street cars in the wet city's speeding traffic
Oh son of a father who doesn't acknowledge you
a pig wallowing in the mud no temporary guest
but brother kinsman
mulling over the origins of his decay

Of course neither would Ezra Pound with his stuttering syntax
false madman without the madman's bitter gall or the thin drool
of firing-squad victims who don't know why they should repent
and don't talk back to me brother of the lowest cur
nor would Ezra Pound switch off the water for good
if you lit up the thirst you've stashed away so long

Now for the slow drink
you've craved like the night

The dark wine in this alabaster goblet
tastes like deep words words oh so deep
rescued by a mouthful of the swollen wind
Aída, Roberto, José
haven't written to me—they've left me on my own—
only Radomiro keeps on giving me the same old song that he drinks
that Johann Sebastian Bach keeps putting on
as much weight as one of those whorehouse madams
knifed to death on the first hostile dawn

I've insulted you enough—rotten shadow—
you've learned much over the years
without digging into anyone else's pockets

I'm sleepy now
Get out of here!
[HSM]

THE TROPICS

Noon strikes
like the shattering of the clay pigeons
in the breasts of the white doves as they fall.

It's just that here everything burns:
the grass underneath your feet,
the leaves in your face, on your hands,
the water in the well that wanted to be blind.

How can anyone think of making love in this fire?

Just the same we even delight in our thirst.

(Give me your hands and some shade,
but a shade gentle and cold, a darkness so thick
even the fireflies have been driven out.)

Panting,
your face tumbles downward, sinking into the moss,
my heart.

Move your side of burning coals away from me, naked one...
[JG]

NAKED WOMAN

I love your nakedness
because naked you absorb me with your pores
like the water when I sink between its walls.

Your nakedness destroys limits with its heat,
it opens every entrance so that I may know you
it takes me by the hand like a lost child
who in you lets his age and his questions come to rest.

I breathe your skin and absorb it, salty and sweet,
until it becomes my universe, credo that feeds me,
the aromatic lamp I raise blinded
when my desires bark at me in the dark.

When you strip for me with your eyes closed
you fit into a glass that rests on my tongue,
you fit into my hands like bread I'm hungry for,
you fit beneath my body more exactly than its shadow.

The day you die I will bury you naked
so that your entrance into the earth may be clean,
so I may kiss your skin on the roads
and braid your loose hair in every river.

The day you die I'll bury you naked
just as you were born again between my thighs.
[JG]

MARÍA TECÚN

Story-book days when you loved me without asking questions
made the city take on the appearance of a toy
when I left you at night I'd walk home with a light heart
through sawdust streets in toy Bethlehems.

In the cheerless trembling mirror of mudholes
I'd stare at my face next to the moon's
and looked for your kisses to stop them from lighting up
the dreams of birds lost in my pillow.

Clay cops and tin roosters laughed at me quietly
winking their still eyes at one another who knows how
and even sleepers green with envy gossiped in their rooms as I went by
telling me you were the Christ Child's girl.

With moss rooted up from Los Chorros de Colón's headwaters
the gardens of the dream with their green freshness waited for me
but your warm fingertips had been a knife-thrust so deep
the tamale vendor washed his enormous naked eyes at dawn
in my eyes' two little gourd cups filled with blood.

Through the tissue paper trees dressed from the heart of the blue
I'd spend the day listening to a band of old archangels
whose cotton hair started new rivers in the wind.

I found you near the twilight later on
—with its tall tree of fire actually in flames—
and in your hands I licked the breadfruit's rind.

Around us flower-cheeked puppets were swilling down
beers of pollen mixed with smoke.

Oh but a few months later you decided to grow up
and with an ugly grown-up look you went away:
since then the city has gone back to its normal size
and in its black stone streets people slap my soul
a sad little boy's who would still like to play.
[HSM]

THE ART OF POETRY

To Raúl Castellanos

Anguish exists.

Man uses his old disasters like a mirror.

An hour or so after dusk
the man picks up the painful remnants of his day
and worried sick he puts them right next to his heart
he sweats like a TB patient fighting for his life
and sinks into his deep lonely rooms.
There buried in his thoughts he smokes
he'd like to invent ruinous cobwebs on the ceiling
he hates the flower's fresh look
he withdraws into his own asphyxiating skin
he looks at his coarse feet
he thinks his bed's his grave day after day
he doesn't have a penny to his name
he's hungry
and breaks into sobs.

But men all other men
bare their chests to the sun without a care
or to the killings in the streets
they lift the faces of the loaves out of the ovens
like a generous banner against hunger
they laugh with children until even the air hurts
they cram tiny footsteps into the wombs of blessed women
they split open like fruit rocks obstinate in their solemnity
they sing naked into the inviting glass of water
they joke with the sea taking it by the horns playfully
they build houses of light in the song-filled wilderness
they get drunk like God everywhere
they set their fists against despair
their avenging fires against crime

their love with its interminable roots
against hatred's vicious scythe.

Yes, anguish exists.

Like despair
crime
or hate.

Who should the poet's voice be for?
[HSM]

MADRIGAL

She was more beautiful than a Czechoslovak factory
when one thinks of her
after being tortured for four hours
in the brightest and newly aired rooms
at the Headquarters of the National Guard.
[JG]

WORDS IN FRONT OF THE SEA

for Roberto Fernández Retamar

I

Belly of the storm and of salt
universe of fish refuge of foam
bearer of the sky we contemplate from the sand
on sudden afternoons when we pay honor to suicide:

you have countless eyes and stinging fingers
like the greenest frozen rats
against us the shoeless the fleeced
against us who have yet to take the final plunge
bold and fearful we come to you
as to the edge of a bolt of lightning

Spill your heavy curls into the ships
swallow the bodies of the traveling ballerinas
trample the dark beaches on the other sides of the world
leave us in peace with our daily invalid conch

O sea let cosmic love flow between us
until we go down into the depths
scattered along the roads of the cindery stars

II

(Remembering Yeats)

I will get up, helmsman, and go to sea with you,
to its phosphorescent nuptials stolen from the night's depths.

(In his garden of drowned flowers
the last lighthouse keeper dances in secret,
proud of the salty rocks along the shore.)

I will go with you, unforgettable helmsman,
where fragrance of the dark shows its huge iodine hole.

(Inside its immense coral reef the delicate splinter
that scraped the eye of the last giant tortoise raises its fragments.)

Let's go, sweet-terrored helmsman,
let the ocean be our unending epitaph,
our widest route,
rough carpet full of stars for an indecisive soul.

(Shiny aluminum dolphin...)
[JG]

THE SIXTH COMMANDMENT

The naked theologians have gone down to the beach
and there's been a scattered surge of terror from the crabs.

(The sea is an old mother sleeping
who wants to know nothing about the rapacious games
of young people. She goes on sleeping.)

The naked theologians toss around a huge white ball
that, when it bounces, looks like a dead fat man
escaped from an eagle's claws.

The little flowers of the sand crunch
the theologians step along like sergeants
but when the sun, red and ice-cold,
slips out of the ocean's pocket
the theologians will receive Holy Communion
each with his eyes on a deep hole of mist
of aromatic mist
visited only by the blue birds
of peace.
[HSM]

WHAT A CRAZY MAN SAID TO ME

You told me your father was a tiny sea.

That the angels were dumb little creatures
yet do much harm at night with fingernails like comet's tails.

You told me the rain is shipwrecked against your house
and your angry sisters castrate the almond trees.

You told me thirsty people are our greatest hope.

That whistling in the park is to confess we are powerless
to retrieve the wine of words we own as children.

You told me the fat woman was a stranger
and that's why you loathed everything she said with her back.

You told me it was better not to go into the street
because it's stupid to cause victims when you reach a certain age.

You told me there's something they call the light
it's impossible to describe with your hands.

You told me the trees are not our biggest enemies
and I shouldn't believe anything they talk about on the other
                                        side of the bars.

[HSM]

MEGALOMANIA

Frederick II was emperor of the high-and-mighty Germans and yet
he was excommunicated by the Pope
because he made the study of medicine a requisite for doctors
before they could prescribe infusions for a fee
or cut off flesh from a person's flesh.

Miguel Servet was excommunicated shortly before
they reduced him to ashes:
they say this was to speed it up for him
to go on discussing the advanced sciences in restful eternity.

Martin Luther believed God the Father's divine liver acted up
whenever he looked through the clouds and saw fat priests
                                                running around
city neighborhoods getting rich from the sale of indulgences
                                                paid in hardcash.
He was thrown out of the Church for defending God's liver.

Thin, puny, with wary eye and down-trodden look,
I'd have to perform marvelous actions like theirs
to be also thrown out of the Church
and save my artless vanity forever.
[HSM]

THE POPE

Grandfather with cheeks like puffy clouds
let fireflies protect your nakedness in its public shell.

Do you know that in the bars they would like to hear you swear
and see you skillfully knife-fight for a woman, nothing barred?

No. You don't know it. Nothing human means anything to you
except your magnificent capacity to look down your nose.

Come along come ride with us in dust-choked buses
walk through the crumbling neighborhoods
visit the pawnshops shaken by the specter of prison and hunger
light the cigarette of the man shivering in the cold
smile in the hospitals filled with running sores
put your arms warmly around those widows
still moist with memories of morgues
granddaddy with all your paste jewelry show compassion just once
without letting the news agencies find out
show compassion next to the loneliness of the many
show compassion before dying and going to that heaven
consisting of glass and cotton founded by barefoot fishermen
by madmen by angry carpenters
by farmers with callused hands and tunics smelly with sweat.
[HSM]

OLD WOMAN WITH SMALL BOY

Frightened hunched over
looking for the last secrets of life
in the ground she walks on
infinitely tired of not being able
to even make an effort
all her spirit dimmed by the teasing of the light
with nothing to forget and everything present
weighing her down more each day
and she blaming her jitters on the earthquake

but he's all dolled up in his spotless sailor suit
absolutely taken with the birds flying past
[HSM]

ANOTHER DEAD WOMAN

My boyhood was a lustrous orange
its fresh gold singled out by birds
by your desires singled out
from the room and its musty smell
filled with knickknacks and shadows
where a huge sour cat was king

But you were old so old
and I was scared of your skin
and your drooping lip with its lilac smear

And see? you're dead now
and I'm starting to sprout gray hairs
[HSM]

CÉSAR VALLEJO

This dead body bursting into flower
—good breeding
raises its knife-edge—
this body not yet introduced to me
better than when it lived yields to death itself
it waves its petals to the seeds of love

This dead body who would have imagined it
defending its cup of storms
visited by blind circus butterflies
its huge pores dead
its old smokes dead from his sitting there
with only its dead-looking roots alive
prompt with the word it keeps to itself
its eternal slippery hand still trembling

This dead body that contradicts me
growing shoulder to shoulder with the language
of a just calamity that crackles

This dead body of dry water
this critically ill
dead body whose bones are guests
comes in runs its fingers over its flags
interrogates its interrogators
this body gives with all its heart the only thing it owns
it wept it comes back and goes away weeping

Somewhere in the world his tombstone breathes
under the solemn weight of the name he gave life to
one day he said things that will always last
the world is much heavier since his death
[HSM]

VANITY

Mine would be a great death

My sins would glow like ancient jewels
with the delicious iridescence of venom

Aromas of all kinds would flower from my grave
teenage versions of my greatest joys
my secret words of sorrow

Maybe someone will say that I was loyal or good
but only you will remember
the way I looked into your eyes
[PP]

SMALL HOURS OF THE NIGHT

When you know I'm dead don't say my name
because then death and peace would have to wait.

Your voice, the bell of your five senses, would form
the thin beam of light my mist would be looking for.

When you know I'm dead, say other words.
Say flower, bee, teardrop, bread, storm.

Don't let your lips find my eleven letters.
I'm sleepy, I've loved, I've earned silence.

Don't say my name when you know I'm dead:
I would come out of the dark ground for your voice.

Don't say my name, don't say my name.
When you know I'm dead don't say my name.
[HSM]

THE BUREAUCRATS

The bureaucrats swim in a stormy sea of boredom.

Behind their hideous yawns they're the first to murder tenderness
they end up with sick livers and die clutching the telephone
their yellow eyes pinned to the clock.

They have exquisite handwriting and buy themselves neckties
they suffer strokes when they find out that their daughters masturbate
they owe their tailor bill they're barflies
they read the Reader's Digest and Neruda's love poems
they attend the Italian opera they bless themselves
they sign strong anti-Communist manifestos
adultery is their undoing they commit suicide without pride
they profess faith in sports and are ashamed
terribly ashamed
that their father was a carpenter
[HSM]

MARIANO THE MUSICIAN HAS DIED

There are no birds now where the piano sat waiting
only shapeless memories of a tremor without a name.

Now the dust is falling
never finding the ebony statue in its path.

The garden gate doesn't open anymore.

At times I wonder if the houses
we leave to die
don't suffer as much as widows do.

At least when someone has sung or
made sweet music in them
as Mariano did...
[JG]

EPITAPH

He showed up on a day like many others
it's anyone's guess

At first he'd drink his wine slowly
in the last bar on that dark beach
pronouncing the names of shellfish
in a way that always drew a laugh
and singing strange ballads none of the poor drunks
could make heads or tails of

Eventually he just hung around
sweaty and very red under the beating sun
he married a common whore—a good woman he felt sorry for—
starting a long circle of silence

His eyes and his memory filled with his native Ireland Phillips
                                           O'Mannion
dropped dead in the street yesterday stiff hands crossed on his chest

without saying a word
not alarming anyone
like someone paying cut-rate for his life

When he was lowered into the ground the ropes snapped
and when the coffin hit bottom the cheap pine lid flew off
His woman—no makeup on her lips—
threw the first handful of dirt right in his face
[HSM]

TERRIBLE THING

My tears, even my tears
have hardened.

I who believed in everything.
In everyone.

I who asked only for a little tenderness
which costs nothing
but heart.

It's late now
and tenderness is no longer enough.

I've had a taste of gunpowder.
[JG]

I WANTED

I wanted to talk about life and all its song-filled
corners I wanted to merge in a torrent of words
dreams and names and what's never printed
in newspapers the sorrows of the lonely man
surprised by the twists of the rain
I wanted to rescue the naked parables of lovers and lay them
at the foot of a child's game
working his sweet everyday destruction
I wanted to pronounce the people's words
the sounds of their anguish
point out to you where their hearts limp a little
make him who only deserves to be shot in the back
understand to tell you about my own countries
acquaint you with exile with the great
migrations that opened up all the roads in the world
about the love still dragged along them
along the ditches
to tell you about trains
about the friend who killed himself with another's knife
about mankind's history ripped apart
by blindness by the myth of the reefs
about the century my three sons will see end
about the bird's language and the raging foam
of the great quadruped's stampede
and I wanted to tell you about the Revolution
about Cuba and the Soviet Union
and about the girl I love because of her eyes
with their tiny storms
and about your lives full of daybreaks still to come
and about people asking : Who saw it? Who told you that?
How can it be done? I got here
before you did
and about all the things in nature
and about the heart and what it witnesses

about the last fingerprint before Armageddon
about the tiny creatures and about tenderness
yes, I wanted to tell you all about it recount
all the stories I know and all that were told to me
or that I learned by living in sorrow's big house
and the things other poets before me said
and that it was good for you to know about.

And I haven't been able to give you more—poetry's
closed door—
than my own headless corpse in the sand.

Mexico-Havana-San Salvador-Prague: 1961-1965

[DU]

THE SEA

THE SEA

I

There are great stones in your tempestuous darkness
huge rocks their dates washed by your shadow
your darkness swallows down even the daylight
left creaking in the cold that comes off the air
and never dares to enter you

Ah Ocean where the hopeless ones can sleep
lulled by your unrelenting detonations
vertiginous alphabet watery landscape that crash into the seawalls
the gulls and the fish-spray are your springtime
your fury is a green pyramid
your weather the resurrection of the intensest fire
the best token of you would be a snail
going across the desert with the steps of a child

(I always loved those quaint villages
that look stolen from the hands of the sea
little houses next to the beach
notorious port towns drunk on saltpeter
hamlets in the fog full of coral forms
far-flung cities humbled by the storms
villages of blind fishermen beneath an oil-burning lighthouse
factories hiding in the mangroves with a long knife

Valparaiso like an immense frozen waterfall
Manta Puna ports of Ecuador that denied me their leaves
Buenaventura aromatic like unwashed genitals
Panama its eyes punched out by corruption
Cartagena forever waiting for hungry pirates
Willemstadt shipwrecked in the oil kingdoms
Tenerife and its sweet cup of wine
Barcelona yawning between the carabineros and the Banks

Naples beautifully tumescent
Genoa Leningrad Sochi La Guaira Buenos Aires
Montevideo like a pearl
Puerto Limón Corinto
Acajutla on a slow beach in my country
everyone watching himself in the solemn mirror the dolphins plow
splitting up an infinity of emerald glitter
with a quick blade

II

"...salt for the sacrifices..."
García Lorca

If night rescues its phosphorescent dome
and your monsters lost beneath the lightning shrivel up
the fish running loose are ten quick children
who deep down ripen the anthem of the scales

When a parade of golden sea horses passes by
the oxygen dead on top of the minerals
muddies the green water with its nasty wound
while the ancient rite of the octopi goes on and on

Salt for the sacrifices corrosive proximity
light without gnawing fire a scalding liquid
ancient pale blood with its furious current
where the drowned men relive their fevers

The sea the sea buries its salty news
and silently devours the solar glare
lifting its face its scar to the heavens
the sea falls shattered into the arms of the abyss

On the docks the smell of rotting fish
and beaten algae deceives us
the sea isn't a corpse it's a battered dream
a mobile labyrinth where the stars tremble

ESTUARY

Today you came down from the black mountain
without your lamp once again.

(You come to me clandestine, like a sweet fugitive
slipping past the town's inquisitive glances
the old women's jealousy as they collapse in the heat
the shouts of the children trying to grab hold of your freshness.)

Naked in the gentle darkness we stayed watching each other
remembering the old days always reborn in the blood
we were more tender than ever making love
full of small talk like never before
all our senses open like a flower into the sun.

Awake before dawn
I see the shape of your body
still held by the pillow.

I've gone out to wash myself in last evening's rainwater
forgetting to sing to the seagulls
as I do every day...

III

A ship
filled with tedium
a ship full of groups of silent people
disentangled from the jaws of the sargasso at a deadly crawl.
At the prow we cut through the great wall of air
and are silent, thinking about the country
where we left love trembling in its primal loneliness.
The books are soggy with seasalt
and from here the water is an immense deserted square.
    So much hierarchy in its battered loneliness!
    Its shivering nakedness like a black stone
    that languishes on the horizon in the wind's arms!

ESTUARY

The swimmers have finished their early morning laps. I'm not in on it.
I open the window only
so the great iodine rose will come to you
the most far-flung and violent rose
that grows everywhere and everywhere leaves its touch

When I see you naked loving each other under the light sheet
—glance trembling beneath closed eyelids—
I know that it's not only this world on the edge of the sea
this keen smell of burning salt
that makes me face up to damp yearnings.

I should never have let her slip away.

I regret it more on certain Sundays like this Sunday the eleventh
when at last my presence means nothing to you
and you copulate slowly
furiously beneath the light sheet
trembling glance under closed eyelids.

IV

The day the father fish prolongs his punishment in the air
the day he risks his life in the lethal air
leftover sea-flowers imprisoned on his last scale
leftover pale yellow algae
survivors of I don't know what plunge
the day my wound lingers on the edge of the sea
away from its widespread aggression away from its volatile
little teeth
the day the swamp is my horizon
and the rose of the wind bends over drunk
you can't
you can't help thinking of the labyrinths we owe
the deep secrets that confuse our hearts.

And the exorcisms don't fit inside the emptiness full
of unease in the middle of an overwhelming dampness
every question sinks to the marrow of the bones
and stays there like the seasons of a luckless year.

Not even all the footsteps could rebel
our thirst falls asleep on us against the dark
and only the nudity of the doves haunts
the ear that confesses it's had enough of being beaten.

(How we'd love to solve the clues or even the whisper
so sure of itself in its subterranean privacy
but what key what bolt shall we kiss
that won't betray us to the guard's face?
How bitterly are we to take the only chance we have left
without letting us slip on the treacherous shoots
pushing up through the ashes once more?)

The sea and the moment are for now indecipherable.

Let's drink
let's have a shot of this bad rum
and get on up the beach
this beach whose sand is a chunk of marble slowly falling apart
and get ready to live up to the dream that draws near.

May 1962

[JG]

THE TESTIMONIES

JUAN CUNJAMA, SORCERER

I

My old skin
snake skin
my skin with its pale hair
holding up under waves of rain
my laughing knife-wound my knees
so solemn in their decrepitude
showing through these rags

Loved but chaste my body
kept a good distance away
from the woman caught in summer's claws
my foot the winner my hoof fool-proof
against the thorns on far-off trails

My grime my proud
loathing for the days of man
my arm and my staff sticking out
like two long-dried-up rivers
my bones put together with ashes and spit
my veins the fire in them snuffed out
my despair with its yellow teeth
in a last-ditch fight against a laughing mask

My love the forgotten
look of the sulking boy
my manly fear
my courage of a frightened man
the weariness that makes me
walk on

II

The devil and god one and the same,
the wings of the dead
make a single terrified sound

All things are the same man has only
to arouse slow powers from their sleep
and take over the deep secrets of life

I know what I'm telling you
all I need is the chemistry
of black prayer to honor your footsteps
for you I blend the scattered voice of herbs
in vials never reached by the sum
I am the only free man
the only one without masters
under my roof of unlit flowers
I sleep in a coffin of red pine
and I won't die this will be my death
one more dream an awakening
simply put off for another time

My body and its wondrous glass
between it and the white worm
while hand in hand with Tlaloc
the real me walks in each raindrop
over the trees and the sea
[HSM]

OVERLOOK

That is a horizon that makes one say:

"I carry the weight of magnificence,
the red plumes of pride
stolen from the nest of fire itself."

That makes one say:

"I am enormous and beautiful,
satisfied with what I can do
like the poorest man
like the most wretched among men."

That makes one say:

"I fear nothing except cowardice,
nothing, except love, brings tears to my eyes."

                          Near Cuernavaca

[JG]

THE DESERT

To Roberto Carías Delgado

The hot wind whistles its nails
packed with dust my dear compadre
it whistles around the black Sonora train
and there's no other dust as close to the heart of beaten stones
as the one I'm telling you about.

When the train whistles it's not answering anyone
it calls together the blind desert snakes
and if it's an hour when the sun beats down hard as hell
the whole landscape cries out for your skeleton
it asks for the rush of your veins over its coals.

Only the dead horse is master here
but when it watches us pass compadre
when it sees us pass hiccuping in the Sonora train
he imagines we're his dead riders
he asks for us as a moist prize
against the fury of the drought.

What can we do compadre
just like God says.
[HSM]

RITE FOR THE BIRTH OF A FLOWER
ON THE GREAT PYRAMID

For Rosa María

I'm leaving you this little mouthful of water
on your summit Pyramid of the Sun
to help you against the noon fire
the punishment of the blazing sun you've suffered for ages

Everyone tramples you and brings you dust
they pound on your huge swollen stone with their feet
they scratch and piss on you in ground-up languages
but who remembers that freshness was your finest ritual

So I'm bringing you this little mouthful of water
the river and I set it down on your brow
to make you smile and pronounce a flower
[HSM]

THE DEER

It has the loveliest eyes on earth, so much like Lisa's. A perfect animal, with a skittish frame smooth as silk. No matter what others may claim, it lives only on water and butterflies and when it's alone it can fly. Its ears came from the head of a serpent delicately emptied out and covered with orchids' petals. Its horns from coral and moss. Its hooves from a tiny bit of night and some ferocity. When it is still very young, it's like a foolish little god and quite touching. In the magic of its youth it is prophetic and arouses sexual desire. In its old age it is wise and makes you drop your eyes. The deer has a woman smell and when upset gives off a sweet body sweat; if this is saved while it's still warm, it's a sure cure against the rabies of wild animals.
[HSM]

PINE

The green monk lifts its austere presence through the fog but whistles at night like a tormented soul. Far off, you can hear the woodcutters' monotonous thumping.
[HSM]

HOMAGE TO SAGE

The leaves of sage that, when wrapped around hot ash are the best bet against a bellyache, contain many magical properties, extremely well documented. Steeped in alcohol they release, when exposed to the full moon, a black liquid that the witch doctors of Izalco use to saturate tobacco. Upon smoking this, there follows a dream of vision and rejuvenation. The powdered form of the sage leaf dried in the sun, taken by sniffing, endows a powerful cruelty and steadies vision. Tiger murderers, especially the youth—it's worth pointing out here—, use it frequently. This same powder, used in various mixes, restores virginity, makes the just man invisible to his enemies, allows understanding of bird language and in general of the tree-dwelling animals, cures fright, cautions night travelers against zones overrun by the flower of drowsiness, protects against the praying mantis, the tarantula and the poisonous lizard, and cures nausea.
[RN]

RELATIVE

I remember it as if it had just happened. He was sitting in his wheel chair rolling his bloodshot, no-good eye as if the lids were slowly and sweetly chewing on it. He had stopped putting on weight long ago. He was going through—physically, I mean—a process of gradual deterioration. Withdrawing into the shell of grime on his stomach. Every part of him—his upper legs, his chest, even his head—seemed to lean, almost sink toward the center of his belly hidden away by layers of dirty clothes. It was then that Leona, his old lover, knocked at the door of our house. It happened at or about seven o'clock on a morning so hot that the recently awakened rooms tasted of smoke. I myself let her in, happy to start the day by opening a door. Leona said: "Where's...?" When she stood before my grandfather, he glanced at her with his good eye and slavered a little. Then he glared at me with such hatred, the likes of which I had never felt before. Because I was next to Leona—who was breathing heavily and looking at him with boundless love from the endless depth of her hunchback—with my broad naked torso that resembled, according to Peggy, the upper half of that exciting God statue hanging in the huge display window of the Paris-Vulcan store. My grandfather started talking: "If I were..." And died.
[DU]

MINOR HELLS

MY COUNTRY'S FAR AWAY

Far from this world, far
from the natural order of words;
far,
twelve thousand kilometers
from where iron is man's home growing
like a rare flower in love with the clouds;

far from the chrysanthemum, from the albatross' smooth wing,
the dark walls that curse the cold;

so very far , where midnight is lived in
and we are prompted by the typewriter's excellent voice;

far from where hope is already left behind,
from where weeping is stillborn or murders itself
before the trash can suffocate it;

far from where birds hate,
from where foul-smelling wolves speak to you of love and offer you
an ivory couch;

far from where gardens scar their own beauty
with knives given them by smoke;
far,
far,
far from where the air is a huge gray bottle;

from where everybody offers rude soap bubbles
and perverse angels drink with cheeky children
all they can of the poison of apostasy against all the dawns;

far from the backbites of the masks;
far from where naked women don't blind you with the light of their
flesh;

far from the consolation of the vomits;
far from the carnality of the pantomime,
from the hangover of unfounded curses;

far, terribly far
from where silk monsters race through the streets,
from where broken forests tremble and run away,
from where each key has a door waiting for it without sleep;
from where the music of gold sprouts blindly
and the unfettered hounds of the cobalt bark;

far, unconditionally far
from where the martyr is stoned to death by mockery
and the saint is a tongue-tied clown.
[RN]

FORGETTING

Last night I dreamed that someone told me: your love is dead.

Your love, the girl you loved when you were young,
has died.

In a cold city in the South
where the parks are one huge dewdrop,
at the hour when the fog is still virgin
and the city turns its back
on the gaze of desperate souls.

And she died—they told me—without saying your name.
[JC]

MIDDLE AGE

Gone are the years of your hot-blooded ways.
Gone are the years in which you would pronounce
certain words with contempt:
cypresses, escape, melancholy, for instance.

You bring your thirst before the mirror
and you're covered with thorns hurled at you:
certainty may smell bad,
you are at last the lonely knight
that you dreaded being, whom you kept at bay
with a little bit of mockery.

Priestly and silent, perhaps,
less given to tears, tougher,
like the good Bread of God the longer
it's out of the oven.
[JC]

LEAVES

Fallen leaves
silent blades aggressive in a delicate way
it isn't autumn who defeats you.

You devour earth
you turn your golden bodies into birds
you burn the mouth of the snow
that soon will die, smoking and dribbling.

We believe we trample you
and really you're the ones who support
our humble stature.

That's why we hate you as much as our heroes:
year after year we have you burned.

And yet, what a huge insult spring means to us!
[JC]

PASSING THE FACTORY

(Mexico, 1961)

While skin trembles under rough shirts
in the nocturnal patio bloodied by a strike
all the ferocity in the world burns in a cigarette
and love, the survivor of storm-driven memories,
is a bird lost in the ocean.

Wind whips the eyebrows of old men
used to watching the struggle for bread
while misery thickens the cobwebs
in their sleepless little rooms nearby.

And I am ashamed of being the lonely man
who simply continues on his way at night
until a moment ago appreciating the quiet
around him and planning to visit Chapultepec
tomorrow Sunday morning.
[PP]

NOW YOU SEE WHY...

Now you see why out of everything you wished for
in those college conversations
you ended becoming an exile's great love

you who were going to travel with the jet-set
to Europe on what you inherited
from three or four honorable old men
you in a stretch-limousine wearing scented furs
you in large silver bracelets
but above all you with the most glorious eyes
in the entire city
asleep now
in the arms of this poor lonely man.

I see the shiny little cross on your chest
my photo of Marx on the wall
and think that despite everything life is sweet.
[PP]

Your face lingers in my guilty dream
wearing out these bitter surroundings.

Come, flower born of the cold, stay with me
until very late,
lend me your blindness.
[JG]

WHEN DEATH

(Mexico, 1962)

When death with its birds
of black foam sprouts from my skin
when my bones question the air
about its rains and its tides
and roots lift their lonely rituals
from my drooping eye
when I'm the one whose place was taken
on the roads the only one not there
to round off the number of footsteps for the day
in your silver body my drowned out words
will still cheer the ripe harvest on.

Travelers in the same cult of love
doggedly we killed oblivion off.
[HSM]

TIED DOWN TO THE SEA

Surrounded by the dirty foam, beneath
the gathered flotsam,
in the middle of the river's forced gifts,
in the middle of its impulsive cruelties,
in the middle of its raw phosphorescences
just hatched with the moon's consent,
face to face with this stretch of immensity
from reverberating iron dock Number Seven,
making great show of the hunger that hangs from my fishing pole,
I see your name.

The water is like oblivion, always there;
the decaying aromas
are little more than needles swallowed in my self-absorption.
I, this hunger and your face,
the indolent sea and the things floating in it,
such is the landscape.

Tuesday, midnight, October?

(When I was a child I wanted to escape
from this sea to the sea in a swift white sailboat.
But the coast isn't the ocean, the coast
has strong nails, claws that grasp you forever
bequeathing you love and misery [love!],
a piece of fabric to fight over, to cover one's bones,
dregs of wine, a number in line
waiting each day for a petal of mist.

Guilt is born along the coast and there it becomes a dream.)

Tuesday, midnight, October, my desperation's
final year—has the poor little thing
been so cautious up until now?

I REMEMBER WHEN I'D TALK OF LISA

One day I was walking through the streets of Vienna
poor like that summer like just another big suitcase
up to Prince Eugene Street
on the learned cobblestones under the advertisements
shoulder to shoulder next to the display windows
showing up in Europe like a clod of earth from far away
that some excited tourist brought home
on his last pilgrimage

Tchaikovsky stirred my soul like a heroic feat
(apparently he was a comfort-loving fool)
and in every chaste door I felt there lurked
something capable of whipping up the flags of my lust

The only thing that now reconciles me with that bitter day
is the memory of an old beggar who watched me pass by
as if I were a naked little boy
and who just moments before had caught me
saying your name out loud
[JC]

A DEAD GIRL IN THE OCEAN

Because you had returned the ethereal body of that girl to me
intact in the dampness
of her death, deep like the slumber of seashells,
and because you weren't sorry for me and my mortal bewilderment
—waterspout in an eye wounded by the old search—
I was the one left out of it, the one with no right to tears.

Now it's late for all that.

What was my crime except love?
And where did she die
except in the waters of my love?

The almond trees injured by the winter's high tides
know my grieving because they fell in it again and again.
They are the green mirrors,
the green comforts of my distress.

The rest of you,
count this lack of wisdom among my deficits of love.

Let my steps, ocean, head towards you,
owner of my dead girl.
[JG]

MEMORY

They were like that those afternoons of our first youth
listening to Las Hojas Muertas My Foolish Heart
or Sin Palabras in the Hotel del Puerto
and you had a simple name
that rang clear when whispered
and I believed in the gods of my ancestors
and I told you sweet lies
about life in far away places I'd visited.

Saturday nights
we walked for hours on the damp sand
barefoot hand in hand in a deep silence
only broken by the fishermen in their lighted boats
wishing us happiness in shouts.

After that we would return to Billy's cabin
and drink brandy by the fire
sitting on the small Lurçat rug
and later I'd kiss the hair you had let down
and start tracing your body with these knowing hands
that never trembled before love or the battle.

Your nakedness flared in the tiny night of the room
and the firelight between the wooden things
under the lamp failed
like a curious flower the one with all the gifts
always filling me with amazement
and inviting me to new discoveries.

And your breath and my breath were neighboring rivers
and your skin and mine two dominions without borders
and me in you like the storm touching the volcano's root
and you for me like narrows rained on
for the first light.

Then comes the moment when you are only sea
only sea with its fishes and salts
for my thirst with its coral-red secrets
and I drink you in with the generosity of someone grown small
once more the riddle of all waters together
in the small hole opened in the sand by the little boy.

Ah love now it's the hour a few years later
when your face starts to become faint
and step by step my memory becomes more empty of you.

Such a small name you had and it was in a song
popular then.
[RN]

THE PRODIGAL SON

Part XVIII

Once again the deep abyss, the old
customs! What shall we do, then, with our laughter,
with our freedom,
with our morals based on anger?

You talk to me about the spirit—an old Sunday theme—, ·
you're lovely and I assume you have a truth for the basis of your
                                                              beliefs
(I can't take my eyes off that squashed insect
and its stomach that ends in a sticky yellow liquid).

Haven't you noticed how boring hope can be?

The main thing is to make a decision:
the murderer's, the person's who dares to be himself at last,
the savior's or the hero's.

You can't spend all your life returning,
especially to the shithole you have for a country,
to the sad mess into which they've turned your parents' home,
only because you're eager to see or bring us words of solace.

Here every sign of pity is cruel unless it sparks off a fire.
Every sign of maturity must prove its capacity for destruction.

And don't expect too much. A drowning man
doesn't ask where the first boat going by is headed for.

But above everything else, there's impatience pure and simple.

Moreover, I warn you to watch your rebellious spirit.
It's the best form of courage
but it can also release rotten sentiments.

We mustn't talk like this anymore. At this point, it would be
hard to come up with a joke or cheer up.

In each side we carry so many dead ones
and so many demons under the skin
that the most serious moment in our life
is when we do our best to laugh.

What's more, our holding on so hard to love is incredible!

The fact is, we've let them cheat us and are so defenseless now
that we can't even make a distinction between our highest duties.
We want to save the lost traveler, the wild beast and the
                                    mountain all at the same time.

In any case,
the efficacy of our beliefs today
(certain gods, ourselves, certain furtive acts, certain hates)
depends absolutely on how fresh they are.
But youth is a savior. The day when the world
has lived enough to be young,
we'll be able to spend our time caring for our children
or being jealous in matters of the flesh.

In the meantime let's not be content to wait.

We've said things that are too serious
for us to just sit here pleading patiently for a verdict.

We're not alone.
[HSM]

GERMAN-AMERICAN HOTEL

Is this, then, the way to forget disorder?

Because breaking free of you of your gardens punished
by the hot sand (always passing through)
is like opening the tap of a pipe that's gone dead
to tease out the last sip of water
before starting to take a walk over fire.

My poor country ay my poor cavern:
you cost me many beasts wounded with exhaustion
too many naked times visited by fear
(after all saying "two lilies" "long decorum"
"putrid matter of violins" "Hegel's barrel"
doesn't wound your lips):
sweet shepherdess of killers
condemned to be green and happy!

They turn on the light downstairs they startle me
but your laughter of a cat who is queen in grandfather's house
can still be heard
silence is not your only culture broth I know it now
the near-sleep haunted by drawn out howls also is
for it you send me angels and snakes
salty mist rising from my tears
voices that speak out like cylinders of gold.

Does even your smell of Lazaretto have to grow like a
                                        mushroom at my side?

You break down shutters and darken tunnels looking for
climates for me to hide in you behead
mile after mile stripped bare only
for snowy nights you corrupt
each quiet summit and how small you grow!

I'm sorry but I'll go on walking
embroidering my flight smiling like every evil I've done
I'll fly
I'll go off to Russia to die to come back to life
or simply to hear two concerts like drums (two)
I'll row very hard on my false passport
drunk with cheap wines singing
some spiteful nostalgic song
I'll go off to forget the idiot I am
unfeeling a blind man who hardly bothers to warn about an
$$\text{avalanche.}$$

When will you tell the difference between roses and guns?
When will you learn not to go into a crazy dance at wakes?
And not to pinch girls while the extermination is being planned?
And not to pamper your sweet make-believe enemies
like dogs you keep safe from disease with a collar of lemons?

(Some day you'll have to spank your soul you nut
after calling it an idiot's soul:
"Lovely soul of an idiot put your butt here."

In the meantime you should be cautious:
all you have to do is weep to find yourself acting the prophet
and
it's so uncomfortable to fill your pockets with proverbs!

After all
the smell of the old mud has been the concern of unconquered kings
who'd still be howling if they hadn't drowned in triviality.

Beware, then, of repentance, as Eliot would say.)

Now they've turned off the light
it's time someone (the Mute, for instance) came up to ask me
$$\textbf{for the rent.}$$

"Why does honesty tremble and, like an assassin,
try to dodge the reproaches of its immortal condition?"

I'll have to tell you goodbye hour after hour
until the word is branded as if with fire on my tongue
and I can say no other word:
only then will I be able to grant myself pardon with enough petals.

Ah you magic slaughterhouse that haunts me:
smile you say to me angrily
taking down your scepter for scourging hearts
your jade harps and gourds and monster's manes:
we were only the ones who spun the pacts
with the screw-up who used to lurk around the best tomb
and now we're the ones who could testify
but we have now stolen the tavern's glitter.

Virgin clouds: go ahead vomit on our shame!
Even the abysses blushed and asked for their sackcloth of ashes!

Horselaughs okay scoff scoff: that's how the mascots sashay
in civilization's grand circus.
But look there's a dwarf next to the exit
with a pistol and a pardon:
they'll accuse you of deserving a prince's booty.

Dignitary
—they'll say—
where did you put your cut of the profits?

Hang on to the scarlet fury
mention that memorable color to them and fatten the chain
(because you're the worst: a malicious suicide.)

They're banging at the door now only mutes
make an uproar like that.
Besides, they're charging me for breaking the toilet's float ball:
I drank a lot last night and patience wasn't spread around equally.

My revenge is to point out the dust the rat
shit and the noise all the insects make
(they escape like devils from neighboring rooms
and their chronic stench of marihuana). Good night.

Ah your meadows where the color of tea would not be appreciated
mystic riches that burn one without wounding
mistress of everything and of my dismissal:
adiós has one more letter than love
that's why it defeats love without making fun of it
uncommon pity in that well
an order with wings of water
of titles of cunning perfect one you become a criminal.

That's why I'm leaving:
my mount was already more than I needed.

Who's talking then? Who am I talking to?
Has someone come with his dirtiest look to make me shut up?

Let my only fault be a certain lack of interest in language
a stunted thorn of music among screeches:
I know that reconciliation would also be devoured
by pale birds called up to be fierce (your only show of love).

Shadow: your age rejuvenates precious stones in me
it returns the most polluted river to its pristine state.
Shadow: just for me win back
your motherly face.

Since loneliness has two big strings and the soul of a spider
I belong to it and am not to abandon it
for any face that's part of the crowd.

Don't let anyone say my joy is like the lamb's:
it is but only because I don't like to wipe away the world's sins
to renew peace without knowing my final name.

What a bad run of luck!
That's why I'm leaving. (I think.)

And for you (the other woman) (body like a doe's about to
                                                    escape, etc.)
I'll say that I worship your secret tears
your grief that would have made warmongers tremble.

You're me myself since then:
to kiss you I need only kiss the hand that touched your pleasures
(of course sometimes it turns into a fist on me
and I pretend to hate you by biting it.)

That park? I hate places
from now on my door will only open for certain circumstances
for everything that only creates rambling abstractions
for fear of tripping up.
The same thing goes for the sonata
and the song titled "Ansiedad"
a black man who's now dead used to sing softly.

Don't you people worry
there are other uncivil accounts I must settle
including one for having saved certain lives
and proclaiming that only necessity is evil.

Oh animal wallowing among sociologies
obsessed by sex: it's your turn.
Do you dance? Confess? Dare? Mix with the worms?
(Gung-ho tours of duty are epic feats Sweaty would say
and death an indigestion of final points: simple rhetoric.)

(Excess: that's the prime mover.)
(But then there would be too many hymns.)

(If waking up before starting to slander were worthwhile
no one would say you weren't right.)

(Ha! No doubt being brilliant is a sacred right
don't apologize for it.)

That's why I'm going
far away
with a taste of hate in my mouth.

(And figuring out short jail terms—to put it another way—
is simply to insist on that pride of yours.)

(Okay: it makes you turn pale
it suits you more or less like fevers.)

(But this will leave thirty countries to account for
while behind you someone has the look of a dead man.)

(Laughing is your fecund sacrilege as a reprobate
—delightful restraint "the discipline of setbacks"—)

(In photographs you have a wet look
like someone who gets up from a piano left out in the open
gambling away ecstasies at poker.
It's just a figure of speech.)

(Gold bullets for killing at dawn
visions of iron objects
creepy things hurt so bad they give off smoke
and become the fruit that envy bears.)

(How weird of you: choosing between Russia and solitude. Hallelujah.)

After all:
Confessing is one of the vices I've satisfied the least I can't help it:
I
the one about to disappear give up
for example
my supply of profiles

my privilege of giving a name
to something that was only going to be a question
I'm giving you up (vegetation and lava) you (flesh forever with me)
I'm giving up the merciful curse
my great thirst for bitter gall
my hunger for minor fainting spells
I give up my giving up things
I mean I give up eating myself starting with my feet
I mean I'm devouring myself
I existed
(I'm just sleepy).

                    Mexico City, the night of April 9, 1965
[HSM & JC]

TAVERN AND OTHER PLACES

I. THE COUNTRY

LATIN AMERICA

The poet face to face with the moon
smokes his exhilarating daisy
drinks his share of another's words
flies with sable's-hair brushes of dew
scratches his fiddle like a pederast.

Until he smashes up his kisser
on the rough wall of a barracks.
[JC]

27 YEARS

It's a serious thing
to be twenty-seven
really it's
one of the heaviest,
friends from my drowned childhood
are dying all around me,
I'm starting to
think I'm not going
to live forever.
[JG]

FEAR

To Julio Cortázar

A solitary angel on the tip of a pin
hears someone taking a piss.
[JC]

SOLDIER'S REST

The dead are growing more restless each day.

They were easy to handle before:
we gave them a starched collar a flower
we showered them with praise on a long honor list:
we buried them in a National Plot
among noble shades
under monstrous slabs of marble.

The dead man signed up with the hope of being remembered:
he joined the ranks once more
and marched to the beat of our time-honored music.

But wait a second:
the dead
have changed since then.

They're sarcastic now
they ask questions.

I think they've caught on
that they outnumber us more every day.
[HSM]

THE CAPTAIN

The captain in his hammock the captain
asleep beneath the animal noises of the night
his guitar strung up on the wall
his pistol set beside his bottle
waiting for the battle like a hot date
the captain the captain
—he should know—
in the same darkness as those he hunts down.
[JG]

IN A FIT OF ANGER

O country of mine you do not exist
except as my deformed shadow
a word coined by my enemy

Once I believed that you were simply very small
not big enough to encompass both
a North and a South
but now I know that you don't exist
I never hear your name on a mother's lips
it seems that nobody needs you

This makes me happy
even if I wind up in the madhouse
because it proves that I invented a country

I am a little god at your expense

(What I mean is: my being an expatriate
makes you an ex-patria)
[PP]

THE NATIONAL SOUL

Dismembered country, you slip
into my hours like a little poisoned pill.
Who are you, crawling with masters
like a bitch scratching herself on the trees
she pisses on? Who put up with your symbols
and your gestures—a girl's smelling of mahogany—
knowing you had been stripped by the rapist's drool?
Is there anyone who isn't fed up with your smallness?
Anyone you can still get to honor and watch over you?
What do they call you now that, ripped to shreds,
you're the whole future in its last gasps in the mud?
Who are you
but this numbered monkey with a gun, shepherd
of keys and hatred, flashing the light in my face?
I've had enough of you, my sleeping-beauty
mother stinking up the night with your jails:
I'm being eaten up inside now by my work,
this stalking that turns the good son into a deserter,
the young dude into someone dead from lack of sleep
and the nice kid into a hungry mugger.

Central Prison, October 1960

[HSM]

THE LAW ENFORCER

I'm old
as old as your hope
it makes me laugh

I carried a saber (but yearned for a machine gun)
among Fernando VII's volunteers
a little liquor was enough—was it in 1842?—
to make me beat to death
a college kid

I executed a guy named Farabundo Martí and Gerardo Barrios
—it happened just a few days ago—
and I cheered Cuaumichín
when he ordered that Fidelina Raymundo be tortured

I was going to write the National Guard anthem
around the time of the Communist leader Francisco Morazán
there was a lot of killing to be done

And I'm still fairly young
hard to get along with when I'm in a beating mood

Blood of your blood make up my age and my memory

I'm from over there, guys,
don't blame me.[5]
[DU]

THE SURE HAND OF GOD

> *General Maximiliano Hernández Martínez, El
> Salvador's former President, was savagely killed yesterday
> by his own chauffeur and man-servant. The murder took
> place at the Honduran farm where the elderly ex-ruler
> was living out a peaceful exile. According to sources, he
> was about to have lunch when the chauffeur stabbed him
> repeatedly for still unknown reasons. Security forces in
> both countries are seeking the killer...*
>   (from the Salvadoran Wire Service)

After all my poor little General
today I'm sure I should have thought twice about it
after all you just don't stop being a Christian
but once in a while the brute in you comes out and you let
                                                    liquor guide you
he knew what was happening after I stabbed him
five or six times
and after the tenth he let out an old man's fart
and slumped to one side of his armchair
he always claimed nobody understood him
and that he'd die like Napoleon one of his heroes
I lifted his face out of the soup
and stabbed him five more times
truth was he was a brave man
the tears running out of his eyes
came from squeezing them so hard to hold back his desire to howl
What made him spit at me this morning?
I respected him 'cause he could be so macho
he always cursed the way women carried on
I think I stabbed him one more time
when he was President he wasn't much of a screamer
the softer he spoke the more the Generals trembled
and the Bishop who was always whispering something
would go off to take a leak
it wasn't for nothing that he sent a picture to General Somoza
Nicaragua's President

where he my dear General Martínez appeared
sitting on a basket full of eggs
I think
he wanted to show Somoza that he could be both brave and careful
'cause what he then wanted most dammit
was not to crack even one egg
what I never understood was that occult stuff
I'd be in stitches when he started to talk in his strange double talk
so much for the occult I thought
God forgive me
well I saw how he stared in my eyes while I searched through his
                                               pockets

he only had on him fifteen shitty lempiras
the house keys two half-dirty handkerchiefs
and a few letters he'd received from his grandchildren in San Salvador
that started off Darling Granpa
he must've taken his sweet time to die
'cause they were half-hearted stabs
now when I think about it I get a bit ticked off
but I gave it to him gently
'cause I thought that's how an old man should be killed
even if he was such a famous and thickheaded man
as my General used to be
others would have been more aggressive
would've stabbed him
as if they really wanted to kill him
but first crunching his bones with the knife handle
not me
if he hadn't spit at me
I wouldn't have felt the urge to kill him
he'd still be there walking up and down with the hose
in the garden
just a grumpy little old man
nothing but a sour fruit rind
but
others
oh mother of my soul

what they'd have done to make him pay
even if it were just a bit of what he owed
others
free of charge
I repeat
would've given it to him really hard
he had some thirty thousand dead to his credit
piled high as a volcano you can imagine
sure—to get that many he had a lot of help
he wasn't the only one
adding them to the heap
he had lots of help
God will never forgive them
what might happen is that God will take his time
or he'll just forget about them altogether
letting the Devil fuck them up all by himself
and that way Our Lord won't be responsible
for all that eye-for-an-eye butchery
which won't keep blood from staining the hands
as someone once said
it's true
and moreover
there are others much worse than my General
a lot more worse
who are still alive in El Salvador
with their tails still up in the air
enough crimes were committed for each of us to have two
the broken down the beaten the starving
those locked up for the hell of it and there were many
and those who fled for their lives: What do you think?
and all the misery in the world: Doesn't that also count?
Of course it counts
since when you confess your sins
even the leers count
my General used to say that money had never dirtied his hands
blood yes but money never
I don't know about those things

only a doctor
can talk in terms of fifty colones or more in my village
when I searched him I said I only found fifteen lempiras
who knows what he did with the millions
that the U.S. lent him
his Invisible Doctors
and his Gallery of Souls weren't much help to him
the knife in my hand went swish-swish
like when you pierce a sack of salt
with a cutupito thorn
sure all this talk isn't necessary
Why now, the parrot asked,
if the hawk already has me in his claws?
I think the whole world can go to hell
because I didn't have such an easy time of it
in my hour of need
no one came to help me
I had all the National Guard
and the Police Dept. after me
and a few stool pigeons from the General Staff
and all the patrol cars from Oriente Province
as if I had knifed
the Savior of the World
God forgive me
out of a thief's simple rage
I did what many others should have done
out of their need to save their honor
or for the good of the country more than thirty years ago
I'm not asking for a standing ovation
but I don't think I've done the worst thing
that's ever been done in this country
the curse of being poor also fucks things up
it's not as if a Barracks Commander
had shot him dead
they've even had the nerve to say that I
had no business in this pie
but now that I've bitten off more than I can chew

I should know that the deceased
was at one time the President of El Salvador
and that is like a bath of gold
that sticks to you for the rest of your life
to touch him
well
it was like touching a tiger's balls
forget the slaughter
that he led in his good old days
after all
that could happen to any President
even to my colonel who is now at the helm
now more than ever
things are heating up
since it looks like the Communists
can never finish off dying
but maybe we'd better cut the talk right here
I don't want to end up talking politics
to a bunch of old
pockmarks
as he used to say
'cause I don't notice those things
actually I'd better hold my tongue
so that my General can go on
resting in peace
if they'll let him
wherever God has put him away
God after all
is the only one who hands out the blows and the rewards
I commend myself to Him
and to the Most Holy Virgin of Guadalupe
here where I am
completely screwed over
for the time being
in Ahuachapán Prison
[DU]

II. THE COUNTRY

The Foreigners

All the Olympians: a thing never known again.
                                        Yeats

*Let an honorable English family live for two years
in El Salvador and you'll have English crows to
dig out anyone's eyes.*
                              W.D. (Winnall Dalton)

SIR THOMAS

In this sunlight
I look like the raw belly of a fetus:
as skinny as the horizon on bare hills,
down on my knees reaching out for a cloud,
full of its color dampened by someone else's spit.

This country is a steel thorn.
I don't think it exists except in my drunken mind,
certainly no one in England has ever heard of it.

Ah whirlwind full of poisonous snakes,
noontime that lasts a century!

To get to the solemn nighttime alive
with a permanent halo,
to be stabbed in the heart
by twelve drunken peasants,
to go down into a countryside of wild beasts
just to prepare one cup of coffee,
all that is absolutely natural around here!

If only a man could hold on to his religion!
[JG]

SAMANTHA

With the lead paint of beauty
spilling out of my eyes,
I know that my life
bustles about
in its magnificent confusion.

To travel with blows falling on you,
to sidestep the beaten travelers,
waking up to steal

the last crumbs of bread soaked in blood:
that is what happiness is,
a kind of pickpocket's confession...

In this sun I think to myself:
"I'm one of Tolstoy's mad virgins
who hops along from one spot to the next
so she won't step on the snakes dying from the cold."
[JG]

MATTHEW

The tropics, an unending fatigue.

The roses in the mountains smell of salt,
just like the bad water we drink in the ports.

And those beetles that smash against the wall,
they look like some monstrous creature's black eggs!

The Mosela wine slowly goes bad,
the Dutch beer grows a nasty green film,
and my best shirts won't last a year.

The exotic novel
is a ghost running through Europe.
[JG]

THE BISHOP

The men of this country are just like their dawns:
they always die too soon
and they are much given to adoring false idols.

A wounded race.
The rainy season is our only consolation.
[JG]

LADY ANN

The gentry are a sad lot here:
who has ever heard anyone talk about
these greasy princes,
near-blacks with huge feet that can't be broken in,
as religious as a street walker,
wastrels!

I dreamt that I was hatching eagle's eggs
but these horrid vultures have come along
to sniff under my skirts
with beaks like knives.
[HSM]

THE FIRSTBORN

I on the other hand weep for my soul:
it becomes full of smoke when I drink alone:
the debris of my soul are betrayed by their master
all for the testimonies of this unceasing machine.
And all that,
while the yellow ashes of my ancestors
are excruciatingly slow as they fall on my shoulders.

We don't know what we've lost, O fellow believers,
in this business about Cain's mark; but
it has to be the law or prayer, absolutely.

I ought to speak of the fog in an unwavering tone,
to make a brief account of our interior lives
(in spite of
and very far above those men who devour
cold cuts reeking of grease,
men too clumsy to kill
or to take the first step in a night of love).

Ah tiniest, bothersome city dangling from my window
like a hanged man!

I'd give almost anything for half an hour
in Chelsea's worst dive (in 1952, preferably):
the gin makes the urinals stink to high heaven,
the old whores cluck among themselves like outraged duchesses
and yet you can point your finger and talk all morning long about
$$\text{chivalry!}$$

What's more I see that morning is now taking over the world
and I've spoken its miserable name:
the little left of the old shadows is what I treasure.
Shouldn't we also have peace
so we can build a wall around my territory?

Because I don't have a big share in this business.

Perhaps I may yet survive this war and find refuge
and even the winners
will pay for my advice:
Natural History has some cases like it,
among the insects for example:
a circumstance that everyone fears would do
—when even errors are simply the feints
of a crushing desperation—
brilliance moves quickly to the front
and your ramblings become a pleasing music,
hope for us to start dancing once again.

Pah! Maybe I'll drink less tomorrow.
[JG]

SIR THOMAS

"The horizon is the least useful thing in all Creation,"
—so my grandfather would say, masking the financial mess—
"One step forward and the whole thing's shot."

And just like that, our toughest experiences
are destined to stink like a rag
in the city's oversized trash bins.
But we would accept death tranquilly
before even the slightest contempt for our little contribution.
Why is there another life
closer to us than dreams!

In the hours before vespers they set on fire the sons I never cared to
                                                                    name,
they spit on my daughters without raping them
(as you would only treat maids who give off a stench
when we lift their skirts with a riding whip),
and knocked over my wine bottles with the swing of an axe
until the earth produced fruit the color of blood.

It could be that I'm stretching things a bit right now,
dreams are so beautiful!
But the important thing is the crisis
that my bruised soul faces at breakfast time.

World: Collapse!
[JG]

MATTHEW
                    (Psalm.)

By contradiction blessed, we're all-powerful, my love.
My opposite self welcomes you, this is how wings let us fly:
this daily tension, then, is a rare happiness that grows and grows.
My sorrow does nothing but shed light on you, a lamp for your
                                                              celebration.
In your silence humanity sings with fervor
and distance makes our bridges take on fragrances.
If you don't listen, the need to seek out your hands comes over me.
If you don't see me, I must insist on becoming a sun.
When you don't touch me, I break into song.

Because you love another, I can face those who are sorrowful.
And because I also love another, you're my resurrection.
Are we like the stone recently hurled?
Yes. And like the river that runs on and on, and knows itself.
You are like the driving force that makes the trees bear fruit.
Let us give thanks that, even being together, we don't feel complete:
this makes us look outward, as through a window.
Let's enjoy each other down to our smallest wounds:
it will allow us to despise the scar,
to give the best corner of memory to grief
and to full sanity, action.
Let's express the affirmation the other holds in doubt.
Let's expect from the other what we don't expect him to expect from
us.
Love becomes a diamond because it had the chance to become ashes.
You make me become like you.
Wanting to hurt me, you get through to me
and my betrayal is your new reward.
You, who are myself.
[HSM]

SIR THOMAS

From out of the eyes of the stag pasturing
in the garden of the madhouse,
from the anise root
that the water's sweet erosion has stripped bare,
from the days when the children
were taking their first steps toward embarrassment,
you come forward, oh terrible love,
as if brought to life by someone long dead
laughing forever on the throne of his vengeance.

I left my sword stuck clean through Charlie's throat.
It was a sunny day in Scotland
where the air smelled like a VD clinic.
I'll never own a better horse.

But now
I'm at the age where everything
becomes a question
and I don't know if it's only because of my memory
or simply the rediscovery of my umbilical cord,
when the air, full of rosy words,
suddenly hits us on the tender part of the shoulder,
in spite of our clothing, made from the tightest threads.

Samantha goes on about planting birches
fertilizing them with strawberry ice-cream,
while she pulls a perfect banana from her jewelry box.
Everything is possible in a country like this
that has, among other things, the funniest name in the world:
anyone would say it's an ideal name for a hospital or a tugboat.

I remember my father saying that with a Bible
and a bottomless pint of Dublin's black stout
he would go on being a Christian even in Hell.
God forbid that I should cheapen his memory
but this New World is an aquarium full of fish
that can't be carved on the altars.

Ah, the old duties of manhood....
[JG]

MATTHEW

The snoring of the virgins asleep in the second class car
slips in even here, in my genteel cave:
they are dreaming of lascivious dwarfs
or of great embarrassments in cheap money deals.
Poor me. I, who mortified my senses to such a degree,
have a herd of swine guarding my new house from prowlers!

Around here even the gardener would feel like a king
with his ass a little sore.

Last night the scent from the moist roses
made me vomit until I bled.
[JG]

SAMANTHA

(Letter.)

My brother, my love:
I really must link spite
to the stories going around about my public life:
"I too have reason to hate this family of savages
disguised as cherubs—I may say later on—,
I too am the victim
delivered in a holocaust for their convenience:
social classes, cold magmas, sketches of real
or imaginary panthers,
your golden labyrinths are now stage sets to capture grief,
unspeakable illness whose symptoms you hide behind."

Night is the best time
for these microscopic plans.
Day is a great old movie
full of moral lessons,
with strangers who recognize each other
and start arguing in code,
mostly in ciphers piled up on pale white hands.

In our old home in Chelsea
no shame could resist a whole evening in my room
(especially after turning on the gas):
I can be caustic without undermining tradition
and death during a temporary peace
is a prize relatively easy to flaunt.

The public show of cynicism quickly turns grotesque:
the soul of a slave, cowardice,
everything helps.

You might say: it's been so many years since we were real lords and
ladies!

Tomorrow, so soon old and apathetic...
[HSM]

LADY ANN

(On matrimony.)

Society's blind heaven:
a man and a woman touch each other's eyelids
as they start making comparisons between their bodies
and the rest of the natural world.

But night falls swiftly
and they must leave the field.
They enter the luminous house by the kitchen door
each one swearing secretly to him or herself
that the venom of each will defeat the other's.

And so the centuries pass, from one to the next.
[JG]

THE FIRSTBORN

Being afraid isn't the worst possible thing.

Fear can be studied like an insect
or like a heap of dung
poking around in it
with a small stick.

The worst thing is to hang on to the bitter weight of the ballast
the sailors throw to the bottom of the sea,
to great applause.
[JG]

III. THE COUNTRY

Poems From The Last Prison

PRISON AGAIN

Prison again, black fruit.

Out in the streets and in the rooms of men, right now someone's complaining about love, making music or reading the news about a battle fought under Asia's night. In the rivers, fish are singing their wonder about the sea, an impossible dream, too good to be true. (I'm talking of those fish called Lily-Black, but actually blue, from whose spines violent quick-moving men extract perfumes that last a long time.)

And the least object sunk or nailed down anywhere is less a prisoner than I.

(Of course, having a pencil stub and paper—and poetry—proves that some hollow universal concept conceived to be written in capitals—Truth, God, the Unknown—took hold of me one happy day, and also that, falling into this dark pit, I have simply fallen into the hands of opportunity so as to lay it out properly before mankind.

And yet I'd rather go for a pleasant walk in the country.

Even without a dog.)

September 9

[HSM]

PREPARING THE NEXT HOUR

I wish I didn't have to think about my fate. Somehow
I associate it with forgotten tapestries of shame and majesty
on which an unfeeling face
(like Haile Selassie's)
would do its best to brand me for eternity. Only the absurd
cold air in this saucepan country of mine applauds
till it touches one's heart at a time like this. Oh assault,
oh words I'll never say the same way again,
place for returning grandfathers to receive their pickings.

This morning the guard brought me only leftovers
—he doesn't know what suffering is, poor guy—
that, together with the fog, have given the day its name.

They're dead lumps of salt from some dead shellfish,
tortillas I fell on with the old fury
that has no other warm places left to humiliate,
scraps of rice as tough as three superb standard bearers
busy pardoning the lives of lambs and crude logics.

The wall is covered with dates I carry in me sobbing,
pieces of final, naked fatigue that scream out and are worse
witnesses of something not even my tears would erase
(terror?).

I've prayed (I am Faust), I've kissed my hands,
and like an old man making his breath bounce off
a cold corner of his cell I've said to myself:
"poor neglected thing, poor thing,
with most of your death left in your care,
while somewhere in the world someone strips down beautiful
weapons
or sings songs of rebellion their wives prefer to jewels,
you listen to honey-sweet marimbas

after you've been spit on by a despot from the provinces,
you hear the rustling of your toenails
growing against the leather of your shoe,
you smell bad (I'll talk more about this somewhere else),
you look for a sign that will mean "you'll live"
even on a butterfly or in a flock of storm-clouds..."

Strict hallelujah, well shouted to the impossible stars,
how beautifully anger suddenly comes on:
huge blade-edge, you mean so much to my soul,
tribute to those sacrificed without beautiful endings,
anger, anger, oh lovely mother, just source of thirst,
you've come...

In the patio, far from here, the sunlight
must be like a white female cat. But am I ready
to show my face the next time they bring water?
Yes. I'll ask for a cigarette.

September 13

[HSM]

INDEPENDENCE DAY

Today is Independence Day: I woke up half rotted away on the
floor — it was wet and hurt me like the mouth of a dead coyote —
with the heady gasses of the anthems all around me.

September 15

[HSM]

SUMMER

I feel the sunburns
("I'm a port far away from here")
of the growing summer:
the reptile's venoms ripen
its secret law,
the blood of things
weighs heavily.
The guards talk about women,
they oil their dark pistols,
they sing...

I
begin to crawl with lice.

September 18

[JC]

YOUR COMPANY

When night falls and a warm
form of peace comes to me,
your memory is harvest bread[6], mystic thread,
for my quiet hands
to give my heart fair warning

Someone might say: what's the foam,
the dust, to the blind man far away?

But it's loneliness for you that fills my nights
and doesn't leave me alone, about to die.

That's what we, the silent many, are like...
[HSM]

I SMELL BAD

I smell like the color of mourning on days
when the price of flowers would make anyone sick
when the poor man dies high and dry
trusting that the rain will come down soon.

I smell like the news of a disaster so small
it's been able to keep the corpses to itself
I smell like an old disorder turned article of faith
its huge flame honored with a Ph.D. in respect.

I smell like far from the sea I'm not defending myself
I have to die of something on account of this bad smell
I smell like a small wake as I was saying
like the paleness of a shadow like a dead house.

I smell like sweating iron like dust set out
to rinse in the moon's light
like a bone left behind close to the labyrinth
under the early morning smokes.

I smell like an animal only I know
lying passed out on the velvet cloth
I smell like the sketch of a dying child
like an eternity no one would go looking for.

I smell like when it's too late for anything.

September 20

[HSM]

BAD NEWS ON A SCRAP OF NEWSPAPER

Nowadays when my friends die
only their names die.

How can I hope, down in this rotten hole,
to take in more than the newsprint,
the sheen of delicate black letters,
arrows deep into personal memories?

Only those who live outside the prisons
can honor the corpses, wash off
the grief for their dead ones with embraces,
scratch up the grave with fingernail and tears.

Not those of us in jail: we just whistle
to let the sound play down the news.
[HSM]

PERMISSION TO WASH UP

I never understood what a labyrinth was
until, face to face with my own features,
I searched the mirror
I use to wash the dirt off and groom myself.

Because here we're more than what we were
near the tip of the airborne and fine sun:
dressed up in blood, prison bars and walls;
the darling sons of mildew, bad smells and rats.
[HSM]

SOME LONGINGS

This proud suffering is a callused privilege,
don't laugh.

I, who have loved till I was thirsty for water, dirty light;
I, who have forgotten names but not the damp walls,
would die fighting now for an angel's comforting word,
for a catchy tune from a melancholy bat,
for the magic bread thrown to me by a sorcerer
passing off as a drunken inmate in the next cell...

October 14

[HSM]

NUMBER 357

The guards are divided into several groups. For instance, those who throw stones at rabbits as they scramble out of the garden with daisies in their mouths. Those who go hopping past my cell, shouting local words and looking at the rain's foam inside their watches. And those who piss while they wake me up, at the crack of dawn, with the light from their lanterns licking my face, and growl at me that it's even colder today. 357, who used to be shepherd and musician, doesn't belong to any of these groups and is now a cop only because of an act of revenge that's not clear at all; they'll discharge him (number 357, I mean) at the end of this month. Just because one night he sneaked off to go sleep with his wife till nine in the morning, something strictly against regulations. Several days ago 357 gave me a cigarette. Yesterday, watching me munch on an anise herb's leaf (I had managed to pull it over to the bars with a hooked stick I fixed), he asked me about Cuba. And today he suggested that maybe I could write a short poem about the Chimaltenango mountains for him to have as a keepsake after they kill me.
[HSM]

SIX PROSE POEMS

THE MORNING I MET MY FATHER

...that father
I have nothing to say about, from
whom I took little more than a
way of tilting my head.

                                              Aragon

I guess I would be some three years old, maybe a little less. I'm sitting there on the cool tile floor in my pajamas because I'm a little sick to the stomach, playing with a woman's hairpin, killing ants and burying them beneath the little dirt I pulled out from the seams between the tiles. In back there's a patio with trees and flowering plants and the morning air is clean and bright, with an unforgettable fragrance that has come back to me several times in various parts of the world, with different emotions, depending on the mess I find myself in. I see Fidelia, La Pille, cleaning the pictures on the wall, with a dry rag; a reproduction of the Angelus, landscapes and still-lifes printed on paper and bought at the Goldtree Liebes department store. La Pille was already old, with her head less gray than a few years later, but gray all the same, very gray, wearing her face of a man patiently, her face more masculine in the huge windows of her nose than anywhere else, except for the little peak her upper lip formed on its highest part. There's a knock at the door, and La Pille goes over to open it, leaving the duster on a small table, cleaning the dirt from her hands on her big dark apron. She opens the door to the next room that faces the street and I hear the strange voice of a man asking for my mother, and then La Pille laughs to herself and invokes the Blessed San Cayetano before answering that my mother is working with Doctor Cepeda Magaña on an emergency cerebral trepanation, but come in please would you like anything even a small cup of coffee please excuse the mess the house is in you can see the kid even if it's only for a short while and if he'd like her to she could even run in the car to look for María at the Polyclinic right now after all if the patient is going to die he'll die with or without the special nurse. At that very moment a damn ant bites me on the finger and I let out a roar like someone asking for attention without even shaking the bug off as I already obviously knew how to do (scraping the bug with my nails and crushing it against my finger or on the floor). Someone picks me up by the arm and lifts me off the ground, looks me over, asking me what happened and I answer by showing my throbbing finger that the ant is still biting furiously, turning its little ass up toward the ceiling. Then I realize that it was La Pille who picked me up and after pulling the ant off, shows me—as they would a chicken that's on sale or a suckling pig—to the man she was speaking to and who has come in here so calm that I am immediately impressed. All I'm doing is keeping my eyes open, while Fidelia holds me out further, offering me up to be kissed. The man does just that, and scratches the side of my face with his blue cheek; I throw myself back looking for La Pille's neck, so I can hang on and hide my face. She says that the man is my father and I ought to kiss him, but instead I act dumb and decide to hang there like a silk worm frightened by its first look at the world. I feel a man slap my rear end gently, he runs a hand through my hair, the pretty blond hair I had at that age and that my mother hoped would distinguish me as a superior being in the midst of the great mass of Salvadorans with dark or kinky hair; and then he takes off my right sock, stripping my foot and holding it between his enormous strong hands, he squeezes it without hurting me, actually I feel warm tickles that tell me that this gentleman isn't as grouchy as all the other grown-ups who aren't my mama or La Pille. They start to talk about things I don't understand. The one who gets the most in is La Pille, oscillating between explosive happiness and tears of humiliation, the gentleman responding only with short words or grunts, and a little later says he has to go. La Pille puts me on the sofa and I sit there quietly with a long face. He smokes and thinks, spilling the ash from his cigarette onto the floor. He comes over to me again, stroking his fingers over my face before he heads back to the street behind Fidelia, who, after many my-God-bless-you's said fervently and the loud noise of the door shutting, comes back to me happier than ever, rattling things off like a machine gun and showing me a very white envelope from which she pulls out a big wad of bills she begins to count, wetting her fingers with spit, exactly as mama would say one never ought to do. In the street a car hurries away with a groan.

[JG]

HISTORY

Written in Prague

THE YOUNG PEOPLE

*"...alarming beings like new species that live
in a space next to ours, spying on our autonomy
and our superiority."*

We didn't hear much talk about the century
yet the sun finds us standing in the middle of it.

We quickly forgot the stink of gunpowder
in our childhood days,
the dry tastes of hunger, the acres of cold, and so on.

History is right now:
we're waiting for our girl
beside the railing of Vaslavski Namiesti
when experience is already in the University and the libraries
and Prague's best chickens
on the Palace Hotel's grill.

Someone brings up dialectics
and all we hear is a loud argument in favor of labyrinths
asking us to forget Ariadne and her savior threads.
They hand us the future and we're fighting it off
like a bat beating us in the face.

We don't want to be pathetic creatures
but we feel old and sick each morning.
Our poets are our teachers:
"I am man, nothing will stop me
if I break with the old life stuck in its pose."
[DU]

A NOT EXACTLY OPTIMISTIC TRAGEDY

Oranges from Cuba in Na Prikope! I don't know why they reminded me of the sweet face of our Rumanian comrade, hear me out, the face of our comrade-functionary-of-the-Rumanian-Communist-Party who attends classes at the Editorial Academy of the International Review (Problems in Peace and Socialism, if you prefer). In the gloomy corridors of the building on Thakurova (which in Czech means, "Rabindranath Tagore Street"), her face like a small Cuban orange, her eyes of a nice young girl and nose of a prince, have become the things I most wanted to see each day. We never exchanged a word (in spite of everything, even though she walked into my office one day to hand me a bulletin) and now all is lost because her advanced, although elegant and hard to detect, pregnancy makes it clear that she married some time ago. Yesterday I leaned out of the window to take a look at the cherry trees on the nearby hillside, and with the help of the sun and an especially high branch I saw that a wild mass of deer antlers had grown out of the head of my shadow. All this is very hard for a soldier of the Revolution.
[JG]

SPRINGTIME IN JEVANI

Androgynous colors, a true Patagonia of colors that jump out at you, a haven from doubt, impervious to the greatest avariciousness, savage yet organized, to be gobbled down in the same way a Japanese neo-symphony is, listened to with your face towards the sun that has just awakened you after the very longest night of love.

The little songbirds aren't afraid of Oswaldo Barreto or me, possibly because they confused us with two workers from one of the sausage factories in Prague. In fact they whistle municipal band waltzes all around our heads, making us ashamed (a shameful shame) for the songs of the magpies and our greenjays, for the talkative uproar of our flocks of parakeets and the earsplitting cry of the hawk suffering through the cold season.

"Beer doesn't go down well at six in the morning," Ingra says to us after bringing us the steaming mugs. This place is, well, a dangerous spot. Enough to make one say at the hour of twilight (even if it's too early to think about it, taking every precaution into account): "Life has been, in general, beautiful." To be specific, it was yesterday, after talking about modern literature's excessively sexual content, that we visited a hog farm. Veterinarians in white aprons checked on the gigantic pink beasts with halfway decent stethoscopes—they were in fact moving—while demanding that we not speak in loud voices. Before entering we had covered our faces with gauze muzzles so that our own germs wouldn't be left behind in that spotless barn. We were told that the barn was even located a good distance from both the highway and the railroad tracks, since each unusual noise scared the pigs terribly, making them lose weight and even bringing on fatal heart attacks. I never saw pigs that looked more like sons of bitches than those.

They're living hams, with horrid little blue veins everywhere, insolent beasts who look exactly like Monseigneur Francisco Castro Ramírez, an exceptionally arrogant Bishop in my country's eastern province. Oswaldo Barreto—suddenly, without letting me in on it—let out the loudest howl that I can remember hearing in the last five years. Anarchy broke out—as an Honduran novelist would say—above all because the pigs started to show symptoms of anxiety that quickly turned into a kind of collective asthma attack. The veterinarians were mortified, running all over the place, and our guide, shaking, absolutely furious, said to Oswaldo, "Silence is the rule around here." "I shout all the time," he answered, "I'm Venezuelan." "In Rome do as the Romans do," the guide recited the cliché in a friendly way but without relaxing. "When you folks come to Venezuela, we don't force you to shout," Barreto lectured him, completely unruffled, before I could hustle him out of the place. I almost threw up from laughing. Like that time I saw the store sign in Santiago, Chile, "Zorobabel Galeno, Tailor," even though I can no longer remember nor understand what was funny about it. Nevertheless, Oswaldo paid for his crime; last night he dreamed he was back in the fourth year of secondary school taking a final in trigonometry without knowing how to pronounce the word hypotenuse. He later woke up in a cold sweat just before daylight and he got me up as well to go out for a short walk in search of a beer.

It was then that I decided to talk about springtime.

The time of the year when even soccer players break into flower, as everyone knows.

And the time of year when Czechoslovakia is transformed into an idyllic command to go swimming among trout or to go out looking for mushrooms or naked girls in the sun that the pine trees filter to the ground.

Tomorrow we'll go back to Prague with our faces tanned by that sun.

Oswaldo Barreto and I have got to leave this part of the world as quickly as possible, lest we start having children with Zdenas and Janas and get fat from the size of the steaks and the extra cottony peaches and strawberries with cream, and forget that someone is dying badly in our ancestral home and has asked for us to come without delay.

But just the same, Long Live the Springtime!

[JG]

THE SOCIAL BEING DETERMINES
SOCIAL CONSCIENCE

The bells of autumn make the first snow difficult.

As if the bell ringer were the devil
old straw doll committed to the flames forever.

Sadness brings on a cough
and if you don't watch out, darling, life
will turn into a day in Little Orphan Annie's life
a crying jag among a bunch of fat characters.

Anyhow, working in a socialist country
and not earning enough to buy a pair of gloves or a scarf
makes me love fundamental metaphysics
wish for its lilac violin to take me back
to the beach where you can have your fill
                              of flowers through your belly button.

Ay it's just that I'm a hack
in the smallest Communist Party in the world
one that will try to carry out its revolution without thousands killed
because the chances for the country's agriculture would be ruined
by the graves.

To make things worse
now you won't give me the little I still have coming
you've every right to say "I don't want to, not yet"
but I feel cold now
and I notice the hole left by my country
in my chest where it would caress me at one time.

I hate your sky-blue dress
your undies so full of tricky strings
everything that hides your sweet little blushing butt

the white stone of your breasts
shaped for the mouth of big little boys
your belly that's the patio where I play with lead soldiers
in the eyes of a perfectly invented sun.

Going out at this hour
washes away all the sins of the world
besides away from your eyes for me there's no cure
for the sight of so many dead birds
—that's something they never say when winter starts—:
I'm as much a near-fascist as Kafka.

Tomorrow the march toward Communism will be one day
shorter cheer up
winter will pull down one more day
in the middle of a very healthy fog
more than one son of a bitch
will go on laughing at the things they say about Che Guevara
and in supermarkets
fat old women will fall into quiet line
to buy yogurt and lots of preserves.

Latin America is a gorgeous anaconda
thrashing its teeth with its tail
and you don't know the first thing about politics
but the story's going around that it has a heart
the problem's how to show tenderness to the waterfalls
or let serenity walk naked
over a carpet of giant parasites
to drive the concept of green from glasses with creme de menthe
and assign it to the major part of the rainbow
made up of wild parrots.

On a day not like this one
thirty years ago
I made my mother a mother
on a day like this thirty years ago

the speakers at the Seventh Congress
of the International were making their speeches:
I'll soon need glasses
and rub-downs to work off this pot
because at this point my figure doesn't command respect
it doesn't go with the story of my famous break out of jail.

Oh golden vision whose name
I can't write down here
the cold has borne fruit in my life:
above all it's given me this longing for you that's political cowardice
and important neglect
of the scowl I've received instructions
to always keep up.

Let me snuggle up in the divine oven
only witches are out there spurring their brooms over the rooftops
all covered with soot and so indifferent
to my culture of humus and slimy crags
(I'm not trying to give you another lecture on nature in the tropics
I want to stay here and sleep with you
make love seven or eight times
till you can't lift your limp arm off the floor
and in bed a world of zinc damaged by acid
is the climate handed down by happy guilt).

Then I'd sing you a Mexican song
changing the lyrics to cheer you up
I'd accept you without the usual jokes
that Sholojov deserved the Nobel Prize
and that there are crucial differences between Soviet poetry
and chewing gum.

(Critical identification with the real world
must go a step further than just scratching your head
and saying the right word for "cunt" in any language
—you can't hear this

144

because it's just supposed to be what I'm thinking
a convention much in demand nowadays in poetry
as well as in the psychological novel—. But let's go on.)

I don't think I should hand you all this goo about childhood
the wild egg at the end of the corridor in my life
instead I should go through the motions of taking leave
search around for my raincoat
crush the last pack of cigarettes
and look as wretched as can be.

The sea's arm is more powerful than the wing of a dove
we're scared stiff swimming in it
but it doesn't help us to fly:
the most down-and-out majesties tremble
when poets fall out of windows, like Caupolicán.
(These are what they call a superfluous sayings.)

I recall now that the bells served to open this chat
but they're useless against your silence and contempt
the bellringer ain't the devil
he's an ass who smells like a sweaty old geezer
and has to go around like me with his salary long overdue
(tomorrow we have another day of Conference
and there's still a good hour's streetcar ride to my room).

Tonight we had no cognac just grapes that were too sweet
(the social being plays ping-pong with one's conscience
especially in winter).
[HSM]

IN CASE OF DOUBT

Karl Marx
awe-struck before a butterfly.

Is that
some kind of confession?

The Secretary General of the Central Committee
sticks his thumb up his nose.

Is this,
on the other hand,
chock-full of human beauty?

This nice-looking kid
(recently kicked out of our ranks, but
still nice-looking)
gets a bullet in the eye
and vultures the world over
ask permission to enter the city.

Oh butterflies to strike one dumb!
Ah the offices of the Revolution!

As for me I'll get me a gun.
[RN]

LOVE STORY

(Documents)

I

The Beginning

We met in St. Jacob's, one afternoon in October. An English organist, Simon Preston, to be exact, had just finished playing Bach's Overture for the Chorale "Kommheiliger Geist". The girl, a tall firmly built blonde, was right in front of me. As climax to one of the many silent waves produced by the crush of people, my lips collided roughly with her bare neck (that day she was wearing her hair up in a way that doesn't do much for her). She spun around to show me all the fury per square millimeter anyone can possibly see in two turquoise-blue eyes. My terror must have been so obvious and of such Eisensteinian quality that it drew a little bit of milk and honey (metaphysical sweets, in other words) from that small mouth suddenly full of indignation; but the girl's face quickly changed and melted into the most inviting expression full of pity and sympathy I had ever seen. And then, trembling a little (in a way I'm taking the liberty of recommending to all who in the future happen to be in a similar trance), I kissed her on the cheek respectfully and then, with a sense of triumph, on the lips. By then the organist was putting to flight—in a very glorious disarray for such a famous choir of angels—the subordinate orders of the heavenly Kingdom: he was throwing us, from on high, Liszt's Fantasy and Fugue on the theme "Ad nos, ad salutarem undam" like a lifeline into the pit of those condemned to death. What's more, a blind man who was near felt around for our bodies and, in dignified and gentle approval, patted us lightly on the shoulder: he had heard the tiny sound of our lips as they separated. A fat old woman, on the other hand, made the most of my absorption to sink her elbow dangerously close to my liver. Someone near us gave off a strong smell of rancid garlic. María (I didn't know then that it was her name) pressed herself against me, rested her face on my chest and closed her eyes. That's how we listened to Bossi's Symphonic Study. We were married that same night after I'd used all my pull in the Party's ranks to obtain a waiver from all the usual delays and requirements. But that night she still slept at the home of her parents, who found the news hard to believe. I wrote a poem filled with hallelujahs, hosannas, and so on.

II

WRITTEN ON A NAPKIN

I raise my glass, comrades,
and first off I'd like you to forgive me
for crossing the doors of emotion
without permission or good manners:
our brother from a far-off country,
the daughter so close to our heart, the apple of our eye,
are founding a noble house on a firm rock.
Comrades, communists both,
they've heeded the sudden call of the heart.
Like work and peace, comrades,
joy is also revolutionary.
A wedding of red flowers,
three cheers for them!
Lots of love for each other!
Forever loyal and mutually supportive,
they'll give us lovely children
(I say this with apologies)
who will stand out on every May 1.
Because from now on
they're each one comrade
multiplied by two.
This, we might say,
is the practical side of romance.
Let us eat and drink, comrades.

III

REFLECTION IN FRONT OF THE MIRROR

Foreigner:
You've made your heart run too fast
without relieving it of the burden of your habits.

She wasn't exactly a virgin
but you can swear that she hasn't played the field too much:
nevertheless,
make a careful note of this sentence
before your eyes:
the next time you get drunk
don't shout at her
that your suspicions crown her
queen of whores.

Remember this well:
you love her very much.

IV

THE PASSING YEARS

SHE (on a Tuesday):

Sadness doesn't meet your needs anymore:
except to make you spit into the waste basket,
cry over the last drop of your precious bottle of gin
and remind yourself not to go to that crummy movie house in
Holesovice again
where Zdena waits for you with her nose as cold as a dog's.
Nowadays you get up very late,
in the mirror your tongue looks white and bitter,
and those famous Hitlerian goose-steps
don't help your heart beat faster in the morning.

It's typical of youth like yours,
much too long, I'd say.
And forgetting is not the torture you imagined:
it's just a flimsy yellow veil
falling, of its own weight, on the aquarium with the orchids.
You'll grow old in the ordinary way,
you'll fight with your children over the thickest piece of the family
steak
and to add excitement to your life
you'll need some Saturdays with Beethoven and Bach.
That's the glory promised in the Bible.

Every 500 years a man is born who's an exception to the rule.
The rest is a question of your pride, wishful thinking.

    I:
A pretty good attempt to accuse me
of seeing Zdena.
Stupidity and lack of sleep
are the only things that bring on old age.
Okay. With my irritating brilliance
and my jumping out of bed at noon
I plan to keep young for another thirty years.
Then I'll fall apart (out of respect for my kids)
and my epitaph will be phony but kind:
"Between the ages of 26 and 27,
a stage that lasted most of his life,
he was the most intelligent man in the world.
Then he got married."

SHE (on Thursday):
Socialism? It's not bad at all:
even the poorest among us
have toasters,
television, French stockings,
good shoes, quality saucepans,
clothes not so long ago the rage in Paris,

paid vacations, refrigerator,
very serious dreams about a small car
for this coming spring,
trips to the office of Foreign Tourism
that are nothing to laugh at.
The only bad thing is that it's all better
in West Germany.
Haven't you heard about mix masters,
LSD chiclets,
powdered wine,
condoms in OP-art designs?
Like every proletarian poet
you have the right to make a fool of yourself
but don't ask
someone who takes off her clothes for you with so much love
to live on large doses of morality
served in glasses of Political Economy...

    I:
    Do you know I could ask for a divorce
    —brilliant idea—
    on the grounds of ideological incompatibility?

SHE:
Don't be scared of words.
Come right out with it: for mental cruelty.
I realize that bringing up those things
I take advantage of a mentality like yours
that believes only in passion.

    I:
    Some day I'll drag you off to my country,
    the comic cosmos,
    the anachronistic microcosm,
    where Cain and Abel
    still kick each other under the table.
    That will be my endless revenge,

the final chapter of this war of love:
your proud Czech tits
drying up among the unappeasable volcanoes.

Of course
to do this we'd have to make a revolution first,
and I, well,
what I mean is,
my doctor...

V

LETTER
Hybernia Hotel, Prague

The wounds you cause are in good health. In other words, their mortal quality remains fresh. On their own, with no need for gangrene or its aftereffects to set in. Do you deserve special credit for this? No more than does the work-shy field hand casting the seed in someone else's land, that's been fertilized for years: he'll never appreciate the fact that, to be born, the powerful tree banked only on a throw of his. Of course, you know I love you. This knowledge is your best weapon and, no doubt about it, you're a brilliant fencer. A sharp aggressiveness, the criminal thrust all the way in, that must first of all stick to the purity of line. But that's not all. If it were, this type of grievance (lamentation, if you want to call it that) would show me up as bitterly hypersensitive, a refined scientific master of the mechanisms of frustration or an idle fool. The worst part is what's behind this: the national arrogance issuing from your pores to dictate each word said, perhaps innocently, by your lips. What a shitty world then, dammit, the one seen from your angle! Naturally, you people are the sole owners of superior qualities and are dramatic, tormented and diabolic. At best, we can try to be funny and pleasing. You and your friends are straight out of Kafka, I and my shadows live in the world of comic books. We aren't capable of certain kinds of climax, not even of a climax of depression. On the other hand, you classify, measure,

weigh and study us. In fact, we don't understand you (you say this in a tone of voice in which I for the first time catch certain shades of meaning I considered at odds with each other: a naive dread of possibly offending, a smug contempt, simple ignorance, etc..., a generous etcetera). The smile with which you never stop repeating "d'you know what I mean?" is always about to "turn into dust and shit". What has become of life, the life in the middle of which we met one October afternoon in St. Jacob's? I can no longer answer you with dignity. And this letter is the beginning of my goodbye, a goodbye that wants more than anything in the world to be civilized and friendly.
[HSM]

50TH ANNIVERSARY

A man steps out into his backyard patio
(where the harsh autumn wind never blows)

in one hand he holds a shot of aguardiente
with the other he gently smoothes his hair

here he turned gray from hunger
and grayer on that day as a hero
among thousands of heroes
here a faint nausea
the prints of one whose young fingers touched greatness
fear
immense joy
all-powerful wisdom

In the depths of the sky shines a star
called hope

he raises his glass
and drinks
[PP]

TAVERN
(Conversatorio)[6]

*Written, like the rest of this section, in Prague between 1966 and 1967,
"Tavern" is the record of conversations heard by chance between young
Czechoslavakians, Western Europeans and a smaller number of Latin
Americans, while drinking beer in U Fleku, the well-known tavern in Prague.
All the author did was put the material together and give it a little formal
structure to make it into a kind of poem-object based, in turn, on a kind of
undercover sociological study. None of the opinions found in the poem can
be attributed to the author alone and that's the reason they are arranged here
without any particular order as regards their truthfulness or their moral or
political worth. The author does not attempt to offer solutions to the problems
that issue from the very nature of such forms of thought in a socialist society.
This attempt may possibly be found in the series of political events that took
place in the socialist countries of Central Europe in recent months.*

*This poem is dedicated to those who saw it develop and grow: Régis Debray,
Elizabeth Burgos, Saverio Tutino, Alicia Eguren, Aurelio Alonso, José Manuel
Fortuny and Hugo Azcuy.*

*The old poets and the new poets too
have aged an awful lot in the past year:
after all, sunsets are so terribly boring now
and disasters, a horse of another color.*

*In streets I'm getting to know by heart
countless bodies are making the eternal music of footsteps
—a sound, let's face it, poetry can never recreate.
So why all the fuss?
So that its dusty echo can pile up
in this, once the courtyard of kings!*

*Don't talk to me about mystery, night owls,
you lovers of golden olden days
for whom the world, it seems, has got to stop now and then:
Has anybody solved the one about the navel?*

He's not saying that to be gross,
and I'm not trying to call attention to his dubious taste,
but did anybody ever really solve the mystery
of that charming little hole?
The way out, much more important
than playing two-sided politics to survive,
load of so much energy stored
in its knot turned inside out?

A DONKEY'S DROOLY DITHYRAMB, HALF-ASSED
GEOMETRY: OBLIVION IS PRACTICALLY THE ONLY SOURCE OF PERFECTION.
AND REPOSE, THE WORST KIND OF ELEGY.

We'd be better off with a round of beer,
a voice loud with nostalgia
calling out for the sea breeze,
a cautious reference to Lucy's tits,
a savage gesture to wipe out any wrong show of respect
around us.

HURRAH! WE CLAMOR FOR A HOMELAND OF SALUTING INFANTRY,
A COUNTRY SUMPTUOUS AND PURE AS THE GLASS OF MILK
A SCHOOLGIRL JUDGES HER AWFUL COMPLEXION BY:
NO COMPLICATIONS, A CLEAN CONSCIENCE, DUTY
TO OUR INNOCENT RACE ALONE.

I TELL YOU HE'S CRAZY: YOU CAN TRUST HIM.

Astrologers are fakes.
Excuse me: I meant astronomers.

YOU ARE EXCUSED FOR NOW, HOLY DUMB OX, CALM DOWN.

Anyway, the times are a-changin',
that's a solid fact, like birdseed:
when I was a Catholic (before 1959) sex was a joke
and hang-ups about the scientific spirit
spoiled everything for me.

Not all its failures were delightful accidents
in the good old chemistry lab,
defeats of my talent in favor of the solenoid,
mix-ups over the function of Santorini's risorius muscle.

INDEED, I PREDICT SERIOUS UPROARS OVER AESTHETICS:
BEFORE THE BEGGED-FOR GOULASH
THERE SHALL BE MANY RESOUNDING WORDS:
BUTTERFISH, THE GOLDEN ORIOLE'S BRILLIANCE,

                                        ETCETERA.

I insist: I don't recall a better round
than right after the Spiritual Exercises
or better chicks than those we made after 11 o'clock Mass.

I WAS BORN A SOCIALIST:
IF WE ADD TO THIS THE TIMES I READ JOYCE ON THE SLY,
MY RIGHT TO TELL YOU THE FOLLOWING REMARK IS CLEAR AS DAY:
YOU REPEAT
IDEAS THAT ARE MUCH TOO STALE.
THE SALVATION OF SOULS, HERALDRY:
YAWNING IS SOMETHING VERY ELEGANT.

Well: that's something else: the taxicab is a great institution,
the only difference between it and summer is the sun and other herbs;
personally, I have great respect for it, in spite of
slight differences.

GOOD FAMILY MEN OF THE WORLD, UNITE!
YOU HAVE NOTHING TO LOSE BUT YOUR NOT
                                        WANTING TO!

Temperament is another crucial invention:
I like it better than calling cards
because it's noble like ice-cubes in an English club,
so much more pleasant when there's a storm brewing in the street.

Oh Lucy, why don't you list me
among the insects you love?
All you have to do is drive a pin
big enough for me through my neck
and mount me among your chrysalises
with a cute little white label: Saturday.
The warm air between your clothes and your tender years
is the ointment I've picked, O mistaken pain,
because rings of invisible smoke appear in your eyes
as if you'd suddenly confessed to being the daughter
                                        of some forbidden cult.
Eternal pilgrim that wisdom has wistfully abandoned
I pursue your truth, beautiful and false.

POETS EAT TOO MUCH ROTTING ANGEL MEAT
AND IF I STAY AWAY FROM THEM, ONE DAY SOMEONE WILL
                                        SAY I WAS RIGHT:
FOR ME CHURCHILL, THE GREAT SMOKE-SUCKER OF THE CENTURY,
A SOCCER STAR LIKE PELÉ
A SHEPHERD OF SOULS,
A LADY JUDGE,
SOMEONE WHOSE AXIS DOESN'T HAVE A SMILE LIKE A CORKSCREW.

In dreams I grow tall in your soul, my love,
and spring does not depend on winter's running away:
my cowardly nature is always chasing after some solution
and on the date set for your bloodletting
it will make sure the night falls in clouds
and all knives have sunk to the bottom of the sea.

HAVING AN AXIS IN LIFE IS THE MOST IMPORTANT THING IN THE
WORLD,
THE WORLD HAS ITS OWN AND THAT PROVES IT:
AH, POOR ROLY-POLY, WHERE WOULD IT BE WITHOUT ONE!

I THOUGHT MY HEART HAD JUST STOPPED!

LETTERS THAT HAVE BEEN READ,
JEWELS THAT DAMAGE YOUR POCKETS,
THE DOCTORAL OWL'S PISSINGS ON THE TOADSTOOLS OF
                                    DRUNKENNESS,

GET OUT OF HERE!

On the walls, frescoes with forgotten dates
are brilliant self-advertisements in praise of beer,
unbreakable morale observing us from underneath the dust (I repeat)
like men's money in a snail's house!

I pick lice from your soul, darling, and from my daydreams
the fickle eggs of lice surface
like the most abject soap bubbles made with a hypodermic needle.
Wonderful: I think
I've lost track of things:
all doors collapse
and the noble vision of your bed grows brighter all the time.

LIFE NOWADAYS LEAVES A WAY OUT FOR SAINTS ONLY
ESPECIALLY FOR SAINTS TURNED GIGOLOS
WHO ANNOUNCE THEMSELVES WITH VILE TRUMPETS
WHILE THEY STRING TOGETHER FORTY-SEVEN WILD PARTIES.
(THAT'S HOW THE BIGGEST MUSICAL GROUPS ARE PUT TOGETHER:
A MATTER OF UBIQUITY, ELEMENTARY.)

Do your duty to your conscience now
(same as saying: "your obsessions")
say that thinking in the shower about Communism is healthy
—and refreshing, at least in the tropics—.
Or pass sentence with all the gall of your young years:
if the Party had a sense of humor
I swear that starting tomorrow
I would spend my time kissing every coffin I could
and giving the crowns of thorns the final touch.

WHY YOU'RE GETTING THE PARTY MIXED UP
WITH ANDRE BRETON!

But where's your tender spot?

NOW YOU'RE GETTING THE PARTY MIXED UP
WITH MY GRANDMA EULALIA!

THE THING IS, WE SHOULD REALLY TAKE
THESE COMFORTING TRIPS INTO OURSELVES MORE OFTEN,
TO GROW BALSAM FORESTS STRONG ENOUGH
TO DILUTE OUR FUNERAL BREATH WITHOUT HARM,
GIVING THE OLD BONE A CHANCE TO BLOSSOM.

Don't look for another road, you nut,
when heroic times are over in a country that has made its revolution,
revolutionary conduct
is very close to this beautiful cynicism
with such exquisite foundations:
words, words, words.
Without a chance to end up with callused hands,
of course,
or a callused heart, or brain.

I'M ORPHEUS. AND ACCORDING TO THE RULES OF THE GAME
THERE'S NO OTHER WAY FOR ME BUT DOWN;
THE FUTURE WE ARE SWEATING OUT IS NOT OURS,
IT'S LIKE THE CHARMER'S SNAKE
WHEN SOMEONE TALKS OF PEACE MAKING MUCH BETTER USE OF
                                                            THE SUN
THAN THE REST OF THE WORLD,
AMONG THE HOLY MYTHS OF PENTHOUSE MAGAZINE.

SMOKING CLAW, BARBED
TONGUE,
EYE LIKE A TRAP,
DEVOURING AIRS,
TRIUMPHANT SOUNDS:
WHAT COLOR IS THERE LEFT?
WHAT COLOR IS NEEDED TO END
MONOTONY'S VERTIGO?

We'd better have another round of beer,
a calm homesick voice
urging speed and at the same time
pointing out Lucy doing a slow dance.

Hey: why don't you really drop dead?
Hey: why don't we make a blood pact,
a real one, really?

OUR UNFRIENDLY SCOWL IS OUR UNIFORM,
TOUGH LITTLE RICH KIDS WITH SPECIAL DICTION!

IN CUBA IT WON'T BE LIKE THAT!
IN LATIN AMERICA IT CAN'T BE LIKE THAT!
NOWHERE ELSE IN THE WORLD ARE THERE
                                ANY PUMAS
NOR DOES THE SUN GIVE OFF A ROSY SHADE
OR ANGER FLUTTER LIKE A GREEN FLAG,
THAT'S WHY.

Everything would be so simple
if a man did not insist
on discussing his battle with good and evil:
potassium chlorate, sulfuric acid and gasoline:
thou art full of grace in thy fragile bottle,
the lords fall with thee
(be it not said with bazookas in the hour
of bazookas),
blessed art thou,
blessed is the fruit of thy flame:
for the problem is not to set the sea on fire.

Okay, but John XXIV's way is still open. (Don't exaggerate.)
I'm not exaggerating: courage is only half of life,
the other half is tactics.

NOW, KEEP THIS TO YOURSELF: REMEMBER:
WHEN YOU HEARD ABOUT THE ORIENTAL SECT
WHOSE MEMBERS CUT OFF THEIR OWN
LITTLE FINGER
YOU DIDN'T UNDERSTAND THAT, LIKE ALL THE OTHERS,
THIS CHALLENGE WAS AIMED AT US:
IT'S NOT ENOUGH TO SAY THEY'RE IMBECILES
I SWEAR THAT IF YOU SHOULD CUT OFF YOUR FINGER
BETTER THAN ME
I'D BE YOUR SERVANT FOR FOURTEEN YEARS
AND YOU COULD TAKE OVER
MY BEST PROVERBS.

SENECA, THAT SPANISH MASOCHIST.

POETS ARE COWARDS WHEN THEY'RE NOT IDIOTS,
THAT'S GOT NOTHING TO DO WITH ME.
THEY'RE ALL WRITING NOVELS NOW
BECAUSE NOBODY CAN STAND SONNETS,
THEY WRITE ABOUT MARIHUANA
AND OTHER LESS FUZZY DOUBTFUL TOPICS
BECAUSE NOBODY WANTS TO KNOW ABOUT THE FUTURE ANYMORE.
AND THEY'RE IMPRESSIONABLE:
IF WE START CHOPPING OFF FINGERS
THOUSANDS OF POETIC NOSES
WOULD BE LEFT WITHOUT THEIR OLD PRIVATE DIDDLER.

LET'S NOT TALK ABOUT POLITICS ANYMORE.

Okay: beets rot in the fields for lack of farm hands.
Okay: let's think of suicide with the brains of sexual organs
Okay: spring watches us from the tip of the best tulip.
Okay: your ideal country would be a forest of yellow marble
monuments.

Politics are taken up at the risk of life
or else you don't talk about it. Of course
you can take them up without risking

your life
but we figured that this was only in the enemy camp.
Or so it should be:
if I didn't louse up when I bought the calendar
we're now in 1966.

ATTENTION, EMPTY-HEADED CHORUS, LET MY LITTLE FINGER BE
YOUR STAR OF BETHLEHEM:
"CATALINA GAVE HER HEART TO A SOLDIER
WHO'S NOW FIGHTING ON THE BORDER...."

*Irony about socialism seems to be
good for the digestion here,
but I swear that in my country
you have to get your supper first.*

NO DOUBT ABOUT IT: HE'S A COWARD:
ONLY CYNICISM WILL MAKE US FREE, I REPEAT,
QUOTING IDEAS OF YOURS.

This conversation could fit into a poem.

WHAT FOR? DO YOU THINK YOU'D SCARE ANYBODY?

*No. The only people who still get scared
are the Boy Scout masters.
and only when it comes to some Central American snakes
called tepolcúas.
I said this because
any blasphemy
reveals its high moral sense
if they back it up with an aesthetic.*

NOT ONLY THAT, THERE'S THE PROBLEM OF SYNTAX,
YOU HAVE TO TAKE A STAND.

*Here's Sartre dragged along by his hair like a sedative:
"To name things is to denounce them."*

THE PROBLEM IS WHAT TO BE:
THE CANCER OR THE CANCER VICTIM.

Lucy and the two of us in a trunk
still savagely butchered
(right, it's better that way, I think).
Lucy deserves everything
and without your friendship I couldn't get through to her.

You see now how war is not the biggest waste:
when the fourth part of a grenade
splits open your belly
must you love the rest of it
that killed the nearest enemy?
I mean, I wanted to ask something better: I believe
I'm already stoned.

AH, CENTAUR:
WHAT ADVANTAGES ARE YOURS
WHEN YOU MEET THE LONE HUNTER FACE TO FACE:
HE LEFT HIS HUNTING LICENSE AT HOME
AND YOU ARE BUT A LEGEND
TO MAKE CHILDREN SHIVER WITH DELIGHT IN THE
                                    MOONLIGHT

POTATOES ARE GOING UP TWELVE PERCENT,
CLOTHES ARE GOING UP EIGHT PERCENT,
STREETCAR FARES TWENTY,
NERUDA IS GOING UP EIGHTEEN PERCENT.

WHISPERS IN DARK CORNERS,
REPROACHES FROM THE GOYAESQUE LIGHT.

SOLITUDE IS INSTINCT'S MOST REFINED
TECHNIQUE.

164

Hell no, solitude's when
the sherry keg is empty.

Solitude is when you live in Tegucigalpa.

Solitude's when you hear the whole gang do a sing-along.

LOOK, SOLITUDE IS A VERY USEFUL LIE. I HAVE SPOKEN.

BLOODSTAINS ON THE FLAG,
FLAGSTAINS ON THE SKY,
SKYSTAINS ON THE EYE LATER ON
YOU'LL HAVE TO DREDGE WITH THE CORNER OF YOUR
HANDKERCHIEF.

Lucy: you smell like some of my country's hot dishes,
I really mean it,
without any coarse insinuations in mind:
there comes a moment when food calls
and if you haven't had just enough wine
it tastes more bitter the better it is, you have to admit.
Lucy: is it possible that you didn't read my letter?
Listen: it can't be, but it is:
O Honey Baby Feelin' Mighty Low.
I bet you won't dance to that, Lucy,
tempting spellbound onlookers to smack
that sweet ass of yours with the flat of their hands.

DROOL OF GOD,
WATER BUFFALO,
STORM BUFFALO:
THE HEART ALSO HAS ITS LITTLE TRICKS:
THE BEST OF THESE IS NOT TO BRING UP CHILDHOOD
OR SIGH FOR THE CROW
AS THE MOST BEAUTIFUL AND FREEST ANIMAL IN
CREATION.

Eat, gobble down your potato
and say that's only eighty percent:
it's raining in Viet Nam
and nobody brings up the subject of hygrometry.

Watch out for snakes in caves, little cowboy,
or for poison thorns:
not for your uncle's cancer or your grandfather's rheumatism
or the chronic headache of the one who brought you into the world.
Small pale demons are brothers of the poet
who will make up felicitous odes to your miserable death.

Shouldn't we have another round of beer?

CHILDREN'S BOOKS ARE THE LAST CENTURY'S BEST LITERATURE:
DOSTOYEVSKY IS A KIND OF WALT DISNEY
WHO RELIED ONLY ON A MIRROR.
HE DIDN'T SET IT UP ON A ROAD
BUT IN FRONT OF THE GAPING MOUTH
OF THOSE WHO'D JUST VOMITED THEIR SOUL.
NOWADAYS HE'D COLLECT STAMPS AND CATS
AND IT WOULD KEEP RAINING IN VIET NAM,
ON THE HUGE NAPALM PYRES.

Does that mean: "insofar as we make
adult literature
it will stop raining on the immense napalm pyres,"
or have you stumbled onto the rugged terrain of the terrible
Chinese line?

Laugh, winter's going to be colder.
Fry, hell's going to be hotter.

I SOLVED THE PROBLEM OF ETERNITY ONCE AND FOR ALL.
THEOLOGIANS ARE AN AWFUL BUNCH OF FREAKS:
THE ANSWER TO THE PROBLEM OF ETERNITY
IS A MATTER OF ASKING OVER AND OVER: AND THEN WHAT?

EACH WORD IS ITS MORTAL OPPOSITE
LIKE MANDRAKE THE MAGICIAN IN A WORLD
OF MIRRORS.

Lucy, cover up those knees.

NO: I'M NOT IN LOVE WITH THE CHINESE.
INTRODUCING THE PRUNING KNIFE INTO THE GARDEN OF OPEN FLOWERS
IS NOT MY STYLE.
NOR THE THING ABOUT THE ERECTION
BEING PUBLIC ENEMY NUMBER ONE
AND THAT PEACE IS ONLY WONDERFUL IN BED.
THEY'RE SUCH FOOLS: PUBLIC ENEMY NUMBER ONE
IS NOT REVISIONISM OR MR. JOHNSON,
THE KU KLUX KLAN, THE ARMS RACE
OR THE TORTURE METHODS OF LATIN AMERICAN GOVERNMENTS:
PUBLIC ENEMY NUMBER ONE IS THE SMOG.

Shepherdess of panthers:
your name will be written in lights.

GET YOUR HAND OFF ME!

ACE OF GOLD: YOU CAN BURN ALL THE OTHER CARDS.

Are you trying to make me say that literature is no good?

IDIOT: DO YOU THINK WHAT THEY SAY ABOUT BIBLES WITH STEEL COVERS
STOPPING .45-CALIBER BULLETS IS JUST A COCK-AND-BULL STORY?

What time is it? The night has a discouraging color today:
Deep down we're all very conservative:
we talk about revolutions and are proud right away
to think that we'll surely die.
Prudence won't make you immortal, comrade,
and everyone knows that suicide cures the suicide....
My God, oh, my God:
why don't You take over the World Revolution?

Except for the Polish bishops, everyone
would be all for it.

I AM GOING TO DO SOMETHING NOBODY CAN DO FOR ME: TAKE A PISS.

ANYBODY CAN MAKE A FLUFFY EGGPLANT PUREE
WITH THE BOOKS OF THE YOUNG MARX,
WHAT'S HARD IS TO PRESERVE THEM AS THEY ARE,
I MEAN,
LIKE ALARMING ANTHILLS.

SLEEP
OUGHT NOT TO MAKE ME FORGET MY DREAMS:
WALKING CHEERFULLY ON THE EQUATOR'S TIGHTROPE,
GOING BACK HOME DISGUISED AS A GREEK MERCHANT.

OF COURSE, TOBACCO IS ALSO A BIG ENEMY
LIKE THOSE PILLS THAT MAKE PREGNANT WOMEN HAPPY:
AND THE CUBAN EDITION OF PROUST, THAT FADED LITTLE VIOLET,
CONTRIBUTES NOTHING TO THE QUESTION OF LUNG CANCER
BUT NEITHER HAVE CONDOMS BEEN GOOD FOR ANYTHING
BETTER THAN POP-ART COLLAGES.

You shouldn't be such a fathead:
any straightforward question can topple you:
give me the names of all the countries in Africa, that black market.

AS BROTHERS IN THE SAVAGE ANALYSIS,
WE'RE OH SO INDESTRUCTIBLE:
IF ONLY EVERY TOM, DICK AND HARRY DIDN'T INSIST ON
MAKING THINGS CLEAR!

WHY DON'T WE TALK ABOUT COSMIC WORLD POETS,
ABOUT THE EQUATION MARCO POLO STANDS FOR,
ABOUT THE ORDER OF THE ALPHABET IN SHANGHAI?

The one sure thing I can tell you
is that the guerrilla
is becoming the only pure organization
in the world of men.
All the others show signs of going bad.
The Catholic Church started to give off a stink
when the catacombs were opened to the tourist trade
and to the shabbiest two-bit whores
over ten centuries ago:
if Christ went into the Vatican today
a gas mask is the first thing he'd ask for.
The French Revolution was a Roquefort cheese from the start.
The international Communist movement has been weighing the value of
Stalin's big shit.

WHAT ARE YOU LOOKING FOR? A PUNCH IN THE NOSE?

I'm not trying to say that we the young
are angels of decorum:
we've learned fast
and we're also good sons of bitches,
the difference is that we enjoy these idle moments.

YOU HAVE TO HAVE A BIT OF MORALE,
DON'T ANYONE HAVE ANY DOUBTS ABOUT IT.
MORALE IS SOMETHING TREMENDOUS
WHEN YOU DON'T FEEL LIKE DOING ANYTHING.

Bring out your bugle, baby doll,
let the world hear your purest intentions
and among other things they'll ruin the night of my dreams.

No, I said that what just crossed my mind
would take me at least an hour to tell.
Art is something that makes us happy:
when Othello strangles Desdemona
he makes us, himself and Desdemona happy.

What's more, the actors earn a whopping salary
and everybody knows Shakespeare didn't suffer while he was
                                                    writing the scene.

No, no: art is a language
(socialist realism tried to be Esperanto:
that was Madame Trepat, Bertha Trepat's thing).
The classic is a stupid dictatorship:
all those centuries to end up at Ingres' violin
(the technique that adorable atom bomb has given us
didn't stop at Ambrosio's shotgun,
let that be a lesson to art).
Lucy: your indifference is bomb-proof.

We communists ought to know finances:
making converts among millionaires
would at least let each neighborhood cell
have a piano, Dresden lithographs, and a vacuum cleaner.

LOBSTERS ARE IN FROM HAVANA, A WHOLE
                                        SHIPLOAD.

And since we're talking about it, let me ask:
the days
that all add up to now: the centuries
of sweet overindulgence,
the millennia of forced joyfulness:
aren't they a kind of obscene promise
made by someone who knows our weak spot?

HAVING FAITH IS THE BEST KIND OF DARING
AND DARING IS SOMETHING VERY BEAUTIFUL.

BUT HUMANITY IS A CONCEPT FOR ONANISTS.
THERE CAN BE NO HEROES
WHEN THE STORM BURSTS
IN A DARK SEA OF SHIT.

IMMORTALITY COULD BE VERY SMALL TINY, IN FACT.

*BLIND APES WITH MOUTHS HANKERING FOR
LIFE'S WASTED BREAST IS WHAT WE ARE.
WE ASK FOR THE MILK OF CONSCIENCE
AND THEY ONLY POINT OUT ITS STEEP PRICE,
AS UNATTAINABLE AS ILL-FATED LOVE
BETWEEN BROTHER AND SISTER.*

DON'T EXAGGERATE.

I'M NOT EXAGGERATING. I COULD ALWAYS HAVE SAID:
THIS IS MARVELOUS, TOPS, TERRIFIC,
BUT I DON'T LIKE IT
(WHICH IS MARVELOUS, TOPS, TERRIFIC).

*THAT'S LOOKING AT THINGS IN TIME,
THE PROBLEM IS THAT TO ME ONLY FURY IS PEACE.*

*I don't want to be the Guardian-Angel-with-Smart-Armpits
but you happen to have the oldest complex:
that of the Glorious
Builder of the Great Pyramid.
You've contributed your grain of sand
and now you want free beers for the rest of your life
—and even demand a proper ceremony to go with it.*

RIGHT NOW SOMEONE IS DYING FOR YOUR
CAUSE.

*We'd better have another round of beer
in this golden hour of chaos,
a trembling homesick voice
calling out for the barroom Mass.*

Lucy: we'd have a great future:
when I'm around you my feelings are just so mel-low.

THE PROBLEM IS YOU'VE GOT TO SMELL WHAT'S IN THE AIR:
GENIUS IS A MATTER OF HAVING NOSTRILS FOR SNIFFING
AT THE CROSSROADS OF HISTORY.

PUT ON WEIGHT AND STOP BUGGING ME,
DOCTOR.

GINSBERG THE POET WENT TO BED WITH FOURTEEN BOYS
IN PRAGUE ONE NIGHT.

That guy's not a queer poet,
he's a sword sallower at a sideshow
—and gee I'd always liked "Howl" so much.

STRANGERS IN OVERALLS, YOU GILD
WITH SACRILEGE THE TIGHTROPES OF THE NUNS.

Okay: all that's left is to talk Zen Buddhism,
it's in now.

RIGHT: ZEN BUDDHISM IS A WONDERFUL EXPERIENCE,
IF AND WHEN IT GRADUALLY LEADS YOU TO TERRORISM.

Oh c'mon, stop pointing your pedantic finger!

BUT THAT'S WORSE THAN ANARCHISM,
I'M ONLY CATCHING ON NOW,
I MEAN, WHAT YOU SAID A LITTLE WHILE AGO ABOUT GUERRILLA
FIGHTERS.
FIGHTING FOR WHAT KIND OF WORLD?

AH, LOST SOUL:
JUST AS BLASPHEMY IS AN ENDORSEMENT OF GOD,
ANARCHISM BEARS OUT AN ORDER THAT IS DYING
OF LAUGHTER.
TO CHOOSE BETWEEN POSSIBLE WORLDS: NOW THAT'S
THE DIVINE PUNISHMENT.

I'm afraid to sleep alone
with that book of Trotsky's on the night table:
it's frightening like a lamp,
like an ice cube
in the spirit of an old man with a cold.

THE MARK OF THE REBEL SHINES ON HIS BUTT:
THE PROBLEM OF INNOCENCE.
ARE WE, THEN, SOMETHING MORE THAN CHILDREN?

WE SHOULD START PRAYING, DON'T YOU THINK?
LOVE: A MATTER OF LUBRICANTS.

SETTING BOMBS OFF IN THE NIGHT OF IDIOTS,
THE WORK OF "OUTSIDERS," SURE MASTERS
OF THE KINGDOM OF HEAVEN.

Lucy, you've broken my heart,
you've left my face forever resting in my hands.

Oh country still in diapers!
Oh sons of Man, yoked to the treadmill,
smiling and red in the face!
There's just about enough money left
for the last round of beer....

My God, oh, my God,
couldn't You be the one to spend the night with her?

U Fleku, Prague, 1966

[HSM & JC]

LOVE

Love is my other country
the primary one
not the one I'm proud of
the one I suffer
[JC]

ZDENA

You're like Antigone, or maybe not,
maybe that's nothing more than a pompous way of getting a fix on
                                                                you.
In any event, like Hemingway's women more fit to be the girlfriend
of an Air France pilot.

What are you doing anyway, hanging out with a wretched poet
even if you aren't the-great-love-of-his-life,
you don't really know him,
although you must have heard them say
he's good company?

He could tell you that naked you frighten him,
that before possessing you he has to ask himself, like Manuel Galich:
"Is this mine?"
And that he loves you only
when the mocking voice of his God says to him:
"Yes, and get going, you idiot."

He's the one who thinks that nowadays Malraux
is a second-rate writer,
that Sartre's not bad,
and that Durrell has wilted in the hands of enemy agents.

And forget it,
the poet will never buy you necklaces:
he'll put runs in many pairs of your stockings, that's for sure,
he'll make you wear the clothes you like least,
he'll even insult you and hit you
and then later make you help
pull him out of his remorse.

Ay, girl,
you were surely meant for another,

someone somewhere committed a tremendous error:
the poet can't help
but give himself over to happiness
calling you (just because) "My splendid beast"
making room for you in his pathetic culture
like the big ugly night birds opening their nest
to the bird of paradise.

May, 1965

[JG]

WHAT'S MISSING

"...as a person, the other has become
a necessity for him..."
                                    Marx

"The classics are interesting:"
my blasphemy, yesterday, after seeing *Romeo and Juliet*.

Today our ration of salad tomatoes increased
and some huge Swiss chard made it to market.

Plenty of bread, enough eggs, rice and beans
as boring as waterfalls.

Shortages make you kind of hungry mentally and
a lot more physically, Fats Flores used to say.

But with hake and a couple of steaks
we'll finish off the week.

What I really miss most in Cuba
is you.
[DU]

35 YEARS

I

But chastity, smelly old hag, shriveled up snake,
guest we'll have to pass up and whom we'll confuse with death,
is a sentence somebody has to serve after all.

Tomorrow is Friday.
Thous shalt not tempt thy Lord.

II

In the smoke of this eternally young day and age
death is one of love's faces.

What's there for me before you now but the bafflement of kings,
the gestures of learning what to do before the swelling river,
the smudges left when I fell flat on my face
into the ashes?

Youth itself goes down the drain
and sadness trots on like a mule.
[HSM]

SUNDAY MORNING

I pick at the guitar naked
in front of the open mirror.

A summer of marked cards
wears on me more than alcohol
more than the throbbing of these temples
that make their peace with discipline.

Oh Red culture, a predicted
horizon, sponges
to minimize the coming days!

Naked Miriam washes
her hair
and the weather returns to mid-August, underwater month.

I smashed that theatrical monocle
because this room is too small.

I'm thinking and go on thinking.
[RN]

SEEING YOU NAKED

For María del Carmen

Minuscule fish of the imagination
naked candies lost
on the stairway to heaven
rough pearls
grandmothers half-opened
salty cucumbers at daybreak
wisdom transformed
How can I enter you
oh collection of herbs and things
put together with the pretext
of a woman's name
and a way of describing
the girl of whom I always dreamed?
[JG]

DATE

For C, in memoriam

Your naked spirit is eternity
let me say it straight out
because it wasn't only water but it will always be thirst
because it had been the danger and the reward
the question answered for the salt strewn over all the beaches
                                                    of the world.

I touched it and it covered me in shadow and light
it broke my wisdom into tiny pieces to be scattered over the roads
it made me bear golden sons and enemies shipwrecked in the ivy
it gave me a new name that echoed like a powerful blow
by the spell-breaking sorcerer on the unyielding door.

Still, I know that you'll soon escape from the grave
and dig a tiny channel to the sea
(to the spot where brotherly thistles
tremble for a future gone bad)
and you'll rise like the beautiful sunrise for those drunks
who forgot their catechism and their filth
on the street corners of the final night.

Rest until then:
without letting tranquility find out
take on a wild animal's strength
and on the burned spine of the autumn leaf
jot down for me the hour
and the name of the beach.
[JG]

A SLIGHTLY REPELLENT BOOK

THERAPEUTICS

The writers prepared a deadly book
for the Honorable President of the Republic.

The President of the Republic inspects
his dagger collection and quotes Pythagoras.

The Honorable President of the Republic
needs a crowbar to get the business at hand going.

The writers have lice.

The Honorable President of the Republic wants
to kill the lice crawling on the writers
by stabbing them.

The writers flee to a foreign country:
their shaven heads gleam in the moonlight
used to cross the border.
[JC]

SAUDADE[7]

Things life has given me
rain-proof horses
often laughing
at my frequent colds

Also a way of being a communist
that the day it becomes the fashion
either one of two things—
but I'd better bite my tongue

Also a heart that goes a little too far.

And a girl who no doubt
must have given it a second thought

On the other hand life took all my poems
written on a kite almost like a meteor
and it also carried off my old clown's outfit
my dumb-friend smell
my smile that makes people feel like crying
and even a little hungry

So
you'd all better get out of my way
[HSM]

EPITAPH

He planted his garden with a bayonette
was cunning and sweet as a con man
his wisdom came to life above all with wine
while the harder he pushed the more luck he had in a
                                      cold-shouldering world
but still his life wavered between hushed insults and resignation

During a week of strikes I made love with his wife 37 times
it was cold outside
and from the start there was no doubt the cops would come

That gut appeared as suddenly as a cough
the gray hairs came on a bit more discreetly
little tufts every ten thousand kilometers

This epitaph was the only thing he still had coming to him.
[RN]

TENSE CONVERSATION

What would you do if your worst enemies
were infinitely better
than you?

That wouldn't be anything. The problem comes
when your best friends
are worse than you.

The worst thing is to have only enemies.

No. The worst thing is to have only friends.

But, who is the enemy?
You or your enemies?

See you later,
friend.
[JG]

TRICK

When I went to see him in his coffin
I wasn't quite drunk yet
he had a very odd look
with his face knotted up as if death were hurting him
his lips pressed together as if he were being brave
or perhaps it was simply the embalmer's work
in trying to cover those big teeth of his
with which he made pianos look inferior
and so I went home with Rogelio Paris
and I downed half a bottle of rum in one swig
something deadly in my actual training condition
Aida was furious and worst of all
Nicolás and Carlos Rafael and the Commandant
watched me show up after several months
of creative retirement from the world of culture
absolutely drunk like before in the old days
I was supposed to already be engaged
in the struggle somewhere in America
but even the deceased would have understood
that it wasn't just another brief parenthesis
in this long and anti-heroic wait
that has cost me several good friends
among other losses
he'd have understood my sudden wish
to attend without being there that backsliding
petit-bourgeois farewell
made even worse by my not wanting to be saddened
by the symbolic death of this symbolic black
his music for two was like a hymn
during our more intense years
a starting point definitely marking an era
more than just any blood pact
or more than *the* blood pact
1962 1963

years of personal experience the dead man didn't know
he went through in the background playing the piano
while we made plans decisions and made love
we drank the foam of our joyous rage
we did creative work and were almost ashamed of it
we made mistakes and were sad about this
and of course the victories so important to us
followed later
we even had time to throw a kind of gardenia on the dead man
("I love this old black guy who sends up
flares of music from pianos
shepherd of yellow herons
breeding tenderness like a demon child")
slightly tacky like all gardenias
especially that bit about yellow herons
borrowed from a set of red velvet drapes
backdrop for Bola when he sang at the Monseigneur
in short I pulled off my trick
I attended Bola's wake without being there or growing sad
I guess I did some silly things and got in the way
of intellectuals and friends
all I recall are a few friendly faces
but when I finally realized that Bola was dead
everything was now absolutely a thing of the past
a cultural news item an event for anniversaries
and I'm glad I didn't turn sad
at the wake of someone who used to fill everything
with fun and good lovin'
[DU]

NO, I WASN'T ALWAYS THIS UGLY

The truth is my nose got broken
by Lizano the Costa Rican who hit me with a brick
because I said it was obvious there was a penalty
and he yelled no and no and no
I'll never turn my back on a Costa Rican soccer player again
Father Achaerandio nearly died of fright
because when it was over there was more blood than on an Aztec altar
later Quique Soler hit me right in the eye
he threw his rock with the most perfect aim you can imagine
of course we were only trying to imitate the taking of Okinawa
but it shattered my retina
I had to spend one month lying absolutely still (at eleven years old!)
I went to Dr. Quevedo in Guatemala and also saw Dr.
Bickford who was wearing a red wig
that's why I sometimes squint
and coming out of a movie I look like a drug addict waiting for a fix
the other reason is that I was hit by the bottle of rum
María Elena's husband threw at me
really I wasn't trying to get fresh
but every husband is a trip
and if we take into account his thinking I was an Argentine diplomat
we'd have to thank God
the other time was in Prague and was never solved
four punks jumped me in a dark alley
two blocks from the Ministry of Defense
and four from Police Headquarters
it was the night before the Party Congress started
so someone said it was a protest against the Convention
(in the hospital I met two other delegates
who'd gotten out of their respective assaults
with more bones than ever)
someone else said that the CIA wanted to make me pay for my
                                                        jailbreak
others that it was really a show of anti-Latin American racism

and a few more that it was simply the universal desire to steal
Comrade Soboloff dropped by to ask me
if it wasn't because I'd touched the ass of a woman walking with
someone else
and then he went off to the Interior Ministry to protest
on behalf of the Soviets
in the end nothing turned up
and giving thanks to God once again
I kept on as plaintiff right up to the end
in a criminal investigation in Kafka's homeland
in any case (and that's why I keep going on about it now)
I ended up with
my Inferior Maxiliar smashed to bits
a severe cerebral concussion
a month and a half in the hospital and
another two months washing down my meals even the beefsteak
was purée
the last time I was in Cuba
I was coming down a hillside in the rain
with an M-52 in my hands
all of a sudden a bull came charging out of nowhere
my legs got tangled up in the underbrush and I started to fall
the bull went right by me but as he was a big lazy brute
he didn't bother to come back to finish me off
it wasn't necessary in any case because
as I've been telling you I fell on top of the rifle
and it didn't know any better than to bounce back, like a
revolution in Africa
it broke my zygomatic arch into three pieces
(very important for the aesthetic resolution of the cheeks)
That explains at least part of my problem.
[JG]

TOADSTOOLS

*I dedicate this poem to Ernesto Cardenal, about a problem of ours,
in other words, of Catholics and Communists...*

"...the forms of petit-bourgeois thought—whether religious, aesthetic or political—are more latent and ubiquitous than toadstools, and more equivocal than syphilis, named by doctors 'the great imitator'... "

J. Longman
(In a private letter to the author.)

VIII

In my last jail I prayed on two different occasions. Inconsistent, I
                                                        know,
in a middle-aged Communist but true all the same.
What will go on puzzling me for the rest of my life
is not that personal concession to fear but something I'd call
the chance happening of extraordinary things. The first,
everybody knows, was when the earthquake split open the wall of
                                                        my
cell. The second was when I was told they'd kill me the next day
                                                and smear
the red ghost with all the shit allowed within the limits of the law.
A guard let me have a Bible for a quarter of an hour: I opened it
at random, venturing on a kind of painful game: and the first thing
I read was this: "He was led like a sheep to the slaughter;
and like a lamb dumb before his shearer, so opened he not his
mouth. In his humiliation
his judgment was taken away: and who shall declare his generation?
For his life is taken away from the earth."
As a miracle, let it pass, Father, but you can't deny
that this was really a dirty trick.
[HSM]

197

IX

I admit that my poetry is not what it used to be, the kind
                                    Father Landarech
liked so much. Good old Corky would insist on convincing
everyone that his pet black sheep was the most important lyric poet
in the history of our country's literature. This earned him the hatred
of Hugo Lindo and other Catholic Salvadoran poets, it earned him
my conviction that he was nothing but a sentimental man
and it earned him the sympathies of some of my best drunken sprees.
I distinctly remember, for instance,
that I mailed him the first love poem I wrote in Cuba.
Eraclio Zepeda and I had been drinking all night and before the first
                                                             light
we went together to wait for the post office in Vedado
to open. It took quite an effort on my part
because Eraclio Zepeda was in love with the same girl
(on a level that excluded any idea of share and share alike,
as we'd done sometimes) and I had to make two hand-written
                                    originals of the poem
under his slightly inquisitorial eye.
This attempt to humor him cost me almost thirty beers
and the worst part is that I never knew
if Landarech ever got to read the poem or if it went the way
of seventy-five percent of my mail to El Salvador, I mean
straight to the Army's Secret Service files.
The poem went more or less like this:
        "And there was no moonlight, no golden sands/and all the
                                    day's dead fires/
had been forgotten./I'd been all alone waiting for you/waiting
                                    for you since
the world's first day./I remember the awe of the huge animals/
and the damp awakening of the plants/on the morning the sea-foam
announced you./I remember the first storm escaping between the
                                    cliffs/

and the first time I pronounced your name./Oh you who are always
banned from my hours/
from my lonely centuries/and from all the centuries of all the men/
who prepared the way for our meeting./Oh belated heroine of my
long wait!/
And suddenly I saw you./Like someone from a race of men cleansed
of all sin/
your perfumes floated/like a garland around your head./
The Light's shimmering testimony/in the middle of the night,/
you were as sweet as the sword of little boy-warriors/
asleep at daybreak under the dew on harvest days./
Oh, adulation of my fevered brain,/love, you have made me a
victim of love,/
may the little shoots of the new branch/be with you./
The solitude of the desert tormented me/but now my bed will
be filled with power./
Oh delightful death of the search!"/

You may say it's charming, Father, but the part about "Oh
belated heroine of my long wait" is something I wouldn't write again
even if I had to do it just to get that girl into bed with me.
[HSM]

NOTES

*"Poetry and Militancy in Latin America," translated by James Scully, published by Curbstone Press, 1981.

1. Otto René Castillo was born in Quezaltenango, Guatemala, in 1936. Wounded while fighting with FAR guerrilla forces in his country, he was captured by Government anti-guerrilla troops. He was imprisoned, tortured and killed in cold blood in 1967.

2. All the quotations of Roque Dalton are from the collage-interview that appears in *Recopilación de textos sobre Roque Dalton*, Ed. Casa de las Américas, Havana, 1986. This was based on several interviews of Roque Dalton broadcast over Radio Havana and others printed in various reviews.

3. For the order of the poems in *The Injured Party's Turn* I've counted mostly on *Poesía escogida*, selected and edited by Manlio Argüeta and published by Editorial, Centroamericana (Costa Rica: 1983). Many of these poems appeared together with others in more than one book under different dates. Their correct chronological order is uncertain and will not be definitely known, if ever, until a reliable critical edition of Roque Dalton's work appears.

4. Ibid.

5. The persons mentioned in this poem are all historical figures.
    a. Fernando VII: Bourbon during whose reign (1808-1833) Spain lost its colonies on the North and South American mainland.
    b. Farabundo Martí: leader of El Salvador's 1932 peasant uprising, during which the Government killed 30,000 peasants.
    c. Gerardo Barrios: 1860's Salvadoran president who formed a confederation between Honduras and El Salvador.
    d. Cuaumichín: legendary Pipil Indian ruler dethroned and killed during an uprising headed by the high priest Tekij.
    e. Francisco Morazán: liberal unionist president of the Central American Confederation in 1830. He was shot and killed by reactionaries.

6. "Harvest bread": This seems to refer to the *wàahil kòol* or "bread of the milpa" offering made to the "lords" or gods of the Mayas soon after the agricultural year in thanksgiving for the harvest and in anticipation of good relations with the spirits in the coming years.

7. The poem's subtitle "Conversatorio" is an adaptation of the term oratorio which refers to a musical composition for voices and orchestra that tells a sacred story.

8. "Saudade" is a Portuguese word meaning extreme homesickness or longing.

Jonathan Cohen has translated the work of Ernesto Cardenal and Enrique Lihn, among others. His most recent publication is Pedro Mir's *Countersong to Walt Whitman and Other Poems* (Washington, DC: Azul Editions, 1993).

Poet and translator James Graham is the editor of *Machete*, a new magazine dedicated to knocking "a bit of moss off the stones of composition." His poems and reviews have appeared in *Cover*, *Bomb*, and the *Hungry Mind Review*.

The poet Ralph Nelson has translated the work of Luis Rosales and Juan Ramon Jimenez. He divides his time between Deya, Mallorca and Kyoto, Japan.

Paul Pines is the author of the critically acclaimed novel *The Tin Angel* (1983) and the *Hotel Madden Poems* (New York: Contact II, 1991). *Adrift on Blinding Light* will be published in 1996 by Ikon Press.

Hardie St. Martin currently lives in Barcelona. In his long and distinguished career as an editor and translator, he has translated Juan Gelman, Pablo Neruda, Miguel Harnández, Blas de Otero, and others. He is the editor of *Roots and Wings: Poetry from Spain 1900-1975* (New York: Harper and Row, 1976).

David Unger is a Guatemalan-born writer. He has translated the work of Vincente Aleixandre, Enrique Lihn, Nicanor Parra and Luisa Valenzuela, among others. His most recent publication is Bárbara Jacobs' *The Dead Leaves* (Willimantic, CT: Curbstone Press, 1993).

my sweet unconditional

ariel robello

Tia Chucha Press
Los Angeles

ACKNOWLEDGMENTS

With all honor and respect to the Creator/a whose guidance has made the journey possible.
I ask your help for the road ahead.

With mil gracias to my mother for never giving up on me.

With love for my father who taught me to look at the world with a painter's eye.

With a song for my family on the other side, in my heart there are no lines between us.

With humble affection for the writing communities of The World Stage, PEN West, Los Angeles, San Diego, San Francisco, New York and Washington DC—you have all inspired me to step out of my shell and brave the work everyday.

With props to my students for their support, your poems are the glue in my life.

With much respect for Luis and Tia Chucha Press for keeping your word and seeing that my words found their way to these pages, I look forward to the work ahead.

With love to my friends whose enduring belief and unconditional love allowed me to see the dream through.

ISBN 1-882688-29-5

Book design: Jane Brunette
Cover illustration: Serina Koester, Ariel Robello and Rhea Vedro
Back cover photo: Justin M. Jobst

PUBLISHED BY:
Tía Chucha Press
PO Box 328
San Fernando CA 91341

DISTRIBUTED BY:
Northwestern University Press
Chicago Distribution Center
11030 South Langley Avenue
Chicago IL 60628

Tía Chucha Press is supported by the National Endowment for the Arts and operating funds from Tía Chucha's Centro Cultural – www.tiachucha.com.

TABLE OF CONTENTS

LA GATA

I drank to drown my pain,
but the damned pain learned how to swim,
and now I'm overwhelmed
by this decent and good behavior.

FRIDA KAHLO

ANGELES ASADA

They are burning the bodies tonight.

The crematorium on 8th Street don't hide its stench
from the staggered silhouettes of drunken men
who spend every cent on brown-bagged bottles of hope
tonight the barrio hums *De Colores* and low rider tunes
as people cope with fragrant asada of human flesh
shielded in hibiscus pink and Acapulco blue homes
these nights a test for spirits stuck in crude oil of fronteralands.

Memo squashes black ants with his bare feet
under an orange moon I trace my name in the stars
we own this hillside view
where ghettos are fallen galaxies
and poverty she is down right pretty tonight.

You promised we would live free... "mas alla de la razon"
and that "all would be alright"
only here, there is no magic carpet ride
no up and away
just Memo blowing *El Rey* on a blade of dry grass
and a German shepherd's ears tuned to renegade radio station.

Tune out Miranda   tune in revolution   baby

Memo whispers wet Spanglish in my ear
but all I hear is the woman next door praying between sobs
hoping God will subdue her old man's temper
Memo can't hear what wars he's survived
her screams like shrapnel won't penetrate his thick skin
his hand weaves its way between my thighs
and Mr. DJ say *all is all right*   *yeah*   *all is all right*
only here, there is no magic carpet ride
no up and away
just a tagging crew playing quarters
on the unmarked tomb of a forgotten soldier.

Hungry for coconut juice and cool ripe melon
we slow dance into K-LOVE late night forgiveness
then make love on an old mattress
Memo strung out on sky, me strung out on fear
cause that's how we collect strikes
at the intersection where first generation and ancient meet
where corn vendors and chrome saddle cement
where shopping carts and homeboys come home bent
and every one counts angels making their way through the sky.

Cause here, there is no magic carpet ride
no up and away for the living
no shiny pennies
early refunds
or middle age
from smoke stack to lung
hope steams crooked, sweet tipped and tender
as the bodies burn I let myself surrender
to the only thing that never changes
my love for the boy who plays Mariachi on the wings of daisies.

SUS CONSEJOS

Mama said, "Latin loves don't last long."
(stick to your own kind)
she knows how hard
to sleep so good
too late for her
for me he's gone
under my skin another splinter
under my sheet another crumb.

Papa said, "You want a doctor, someone to take care of you."
(stick to your own kind)
he knows how hard to slap
brown on white won't stick
he knew he'd quit
he knew love lies
in my bed
under my skin
sticking not stuck.

"Stick to your own kind, m'ija."
I know to last
I must deny love of self
to find my kind
I know they said they know what's best
but still I make my love in mud.

HOME

where I'm from real people eat tacos at 4 a.m.
drunk and high they enjoy freedom of D

                                    R

                                  O

                                    P top

low
low
low riders
with neon bass and no where
no where to go
real people lie steal and smoke their lives away
angry and undereducated
real people need drama and day jobs
to occupy voids between hangovers
and month late car payments

confined to waiting rooms
real people stare down
real people under florescent lights
they print their names at the X with a lucky pen
for a chance at free checking and chest exams

with security cameras watching
real people dance with mannequins
after closing real people sweat
under heat lamps their bodies melding
into one seamless happy ending

once a flaming rabbit's foot
fell through the black top
of my real world
the roof
the roof
the roof is on fire
it was the first time

i.   la gata loca
saw a hole to the other side
where the best years of real life
were worth more than a slow dance with number 33
on the all star team

for me the thunder of my feet
pounding what's real into molehills behind me
is as loud as the night I decided to hunt the wildebeest of more

LET ME RIDE

let me ride in the lover's car
where I am Iztaccihuatl on his lap
white volcano before war
bass rumbling below us
warnings from fault lines undecided
which side we'll choose

it takes an hour to go one mile down the Strip
that is three lights
his fingers tapping Morse code inside
the lover's car where bras are left like surrender flags
and perfect bald heads grow wet with cinnamon kisses

I want to be the Aztec calendar girl
mounted between his shrine to la Virgin and Teena Marie
hickeys framing my charm necklace
laughing at bullhorn warnings
from policemen too afraid to talk shit to our faces

it is before curfew, graduation and Uncle Sam's nagging plea
to be all you can be on this night
you must ride, 15 mph, detailed and louder than your neighbor
you must know which hand signs peace and which will launch wanton action
you must bite down hard on your urge to outrun
every other hard shell in the race

let me ride backseat immune to stop signs
pilfering seconds before life calls
before we become hazy interpretations of what they'd have us be
before laptops and DSL, Afghanistan and dress pants
before credit checks, regrets, training camps, freshman politics, rudimentary
skills we'll need to survive after this night
steady driver, we're making time stand still back here
steady, we're undressing worm holes back here
steady, we ain't ready to go home just yet

TUFF MEDICINE

Oye nena!
this poem is tuff medicine
made up of 2 parts naked storm
3 part mercenary men
4 part petalpusher
1 part oxygen

I dub dub dare ya
become electric buttafly
come on sour angel stop frontin
you holdin up traffic in your veins
you slumlordin your soul

precious peahen penned into your "Stories"
dying to dig up roots of someone else's pain
no one won here
worse yet
no one ever will

dig this vision
one twelve foot neon WIC sign
it took six men to climb the pole
black birds with fat bellies
to align the holes
just right   all day   all night
you keep your Venus intact
cry anti-freeze
when he's late to your 3 a.m. dream
the one when you ride Coney Island's *Earthquake*
10 times in a row
shaken from outside-in
you find a way to forgive

from top twin tenement towers
Big Boi screams   *Perdoname!*
into a universal megaphone
they come quick
take him in for inciting a riot

it takes life to live here
steady hands to hold the rails

child I dub dub dare ya
play the panic down
calm your tracks with cocoa butta
and become sweet face of nowhere

THE NIGHT THE DJ SAVED MY LIFE

for New York after hours

his eyes split the dance floor

his lips split the groove of my smile
his vinyl smooth caress took one breast and fed an island nation
between the ebb and his tongue
a spinning table of reasons
why not
come
undone

we stood erect
pulsing time into timba
laughter then dip into back board marimba
equal shots of mambo & lime
his finger epidermal needles
retracting inhibition from my spine
in   slow   slide   scratch
we held our breath exhaled and came in time

sigh   all that's left of the DJ that saved my life
is a mixed tape and over 18 glowing under black light

RAVE POLITICS

you can look but don't touch the butterflies
an angel is a death trap with wings
space aliens are open to solicitations
white pills will make your skin peel off
the blue ones will put it back on
don't take a first date
if your friends multiply before your eyes
take off the glasses
if they grow another head
gently push it back in
a bad dancer is probably a Narc
not everybabydoe is looking at you
two is boring
three or more is showbiz
when you take off in the red balloon don't look down
when you land   don't look up
fire-breathing dragons will deflate
when driving into nowhere gas up and buy tic tacs
to   t r a i l   behind you
if glass shards spin all around
pretend they're sugar plum fairies
but whatever you do never
no never stop dancing

RAPPER'S DELIGHT

hello of cleavage
cinch of stretch denim
poison sprayed cross your ass & chest

against the wall you a Malaysian carving
invisible basket of dreams balanced on your head
your curves calling men to reel you in

the back seat a sweat lodge
frost of nights you called home from pay phone
half whimper half spit
left because you wouldn't —
no couldn't — why do you resist?

and how they scorned your rebellion
threw the mic in your face
back stage a race to the after party
where they took turns inside you
while you'd wait for your Savior to come

in hotel lobby they'd rub reason and meter
in your ears a buzz of something you had to say
burning behind your teeth a wad of gum
clicking tongue of paces

you blew on the dice
won a shadow deal behind emcee of the week
graduate of street games (invented and real)
emory board routine on acrylic nails
filing holes in your head heart womb
where poem or love or baby might have grown
had you'd owned your free will

against the wall you look angelic
wide-eyed with magnetic pull of spotlights
high of his hand moving up your thigh

see girl, a rapper's delight always delivers sunshine
until she's sent home at sunrise black-eyed and broken

THE RUNWAY

Hailey's comet tears down La Cienega Blvd.
splitting the car wash
open like a hooker's thighs

blisters rise on Randy's giant doughnut
sweet confections and garbage men
scramble for their lives

the unfortunate driver
stuck at the eternal red light
glass cut palms
a lifetime of gripping the wheel
too tight

the misunderstood sky
a field of bloody salutations
waving hello

goodbye.

IN YOUR FACE LOVE

trapped in cul-de-sacs and Denny's bathrooms
the loyal are tested to see how much split your bottom lip can take
on the other side of love is a brown boy
who never meant to hurt you

asleep in alleys and on stained sheets at Motel 6
the one between Pal's Happy Liquor and Emerald City Express
with noodles and malt beer to fill the dying beast
in your face love forgets which hand struck first
who did what when and why even friends don't question no more

spider web in the corner
prey tired and sufficiently numb
the hourglass on your neck
accessory to a crime you'll claim you like it rough
each welt proof enough
you're no body 'til somebody loves you

in your face love like the first 18 days in Vietnam
a lifetime of seizures
virgin nostrils in a field of rusty poppies
like winter in Belgrade and summer in Harlem
in your face love's a lightening rod in the grip of an iron man
a covenant of Sunday slow jams
a Rolls Royce in quick sand
in your face love is La Motta vs. Sugar Ray 1951
in the 13th round saying I never went down
no, for this love I stood standing

CARTA PERSONAL

Abuelita's hands wake me
soft as masa they tell of maquiladora murders
young girls left crumpled, braids cut off
bits of pay slips found under pink nails
they warn of an invisible plague that has invaded my mother
red armies taking over honest cells.

Glaring pixels blind eyes too tired to sleep
as the dial up begins my fingers lament the deserts between us
under each key a child's skull from the graves of Monzote
under each rock the echo of two 4th graders at war
their scissors still chasing each other around Room 11
with a hate as open and hungry as the Grand Canyon.

My sweet unconditional,
what of the woman who changed her name to Lola
boarded a Greyhound and crossed state-after-state to see
if she'd make the same mistakes as far from him as she could get
and what of lovers hunted by mosquitoes in Managua
their dark flesh hidden by banana leaves
depressed breezes flirting with their nipples
will the scars of their scratching show come dawn?

What of the screams of the mute
do they leave from the eyes
and do those same eyes extract memory from tears
enough to start a new blue planet
those piercing red layers of granite between us
like the painted walls of Palenque
what amount of dynamite would it take to break into a heart that stiff?

My sweet unconditional,
there is no one to send these questions to but you

tonight an anonymous brick went through the window of Mr. Lim's market
landing one shoplifter dead.
My love do curses brand the same in Korean
and if they do where can we market this rage?
There is sadness at 3 a.m. at 4 and at 5
there is dawn then duty
pinned to my mattress
tattooed to last night's neck
spelled in pink crosses along the ravine
our love, an s.o.s. straddled over time.

OVER PASS-T DUE CONFESSION

I.

Under the overpass two boys walked
parading gold-dipped silver chains
breast plate crosses & Nike signs, size of sunspots
enough to catch the eye of our would-be leader

II.

I knew the short one from Kindergarten
where we shared a box
his name on top
and I'd hated him for it

a good girl would have looked away
when the tall one's veins burst
frightened moons covered with webs of red licorice
a good girl would have ran when his kneecaps shattered
sound like lunar rover landing

III.

today there are HBO specials
that could make this suburban horror real for you non-believers
this perennial fuck you at the hand of a practice bat
from have not to have less fools

IV.

"e'ry-body deserves a good beat down once in awhile"
that's what they told me and that's what I sold my God
after all *my man* was most beautiful when he'd hit his mark
and sad girls that want to stay happy learn to laugh shit off

V.

shamed I think of the sons I don't have
the ones I dare teach
wound collars of barbed wire nailed to their necks
an ancient scar size of dime bag
settle between their brow
I think of the Amor-all slide that made it easy
to jump in and get away

VI.

Hell is that they went on living
with grandma's waffles and football
to make the work week sweeter
they went on drinking at 4th St. Dicks
planning their revenge on napkins and place mats
but we were a faceless plague
spreading ourselves too thin

VII.

so I laughed the scales
up and down the white ivory of the poor bastard's teeth
my apologies for having nothing better to do that night
than hold my man's chain
while he worked out his rage on the face of someone else's brother

RICO SUAVE

Rico *Suave* liked to lick muñeca virgins
enough to get them loose
and when they closed their eyes
he would slip
bonitas
queridas
and *suavecitas*
down their skirts
let the bass in his Camero do most of the work
while his hands kept time on drumskin hips
their breast like burial mounds
pressed against his black curls
they'd kiss
taste God
swear faith
flower panties drop to the floor
knees deep in zebra print
Suave, el santo, reclined on his throne
a crushed velvet cushion to lean on
while pushing religion down their throats.

THE PREACHER AT VICTORY OUTREACH SPEAKS TO SAVE MY HOMEBOY'S SOUL

Sinner beware!!
Submit your sin at the feet of Jesus
polish God's shoes with your retired rag
run boys, run round the snake-charmed congregation
your arms raised and chest cocked like Black Mambo.

Spread the word children
with razor sharp prayers let the world know
the homeboy crusade is coming
high as bonfire flame
aiming for your Saturdays and Mondays
in between days
claiming your families as their own.

Visitors, slouching in the back row
we see you, sloppy with the Devil's lies
we've known you as temptation
but not this time
today you are in *Our* house.

My sons, know you are here to suffer
let me carve out your tattoos
letter by letter
until the warrior has been scarred over
until you are a callous of regret and misguided good intentions.

Get a job good citizen
break the Lord off some pocket change
there is Kool-Aid and donuts in the vestibule for members.
Did you bring your ID?
Have your children memorized their Psalm?
Is your wife alone at home?

Brothers, we'll bail you out of your spiritual prison
we'll mortgage your soul
come, lend me your hand
let the Holy Spirit take hold your tongue
don't fight the work of redemption
there is a Heaven right here on Earth
and Vatos are more than welcome.

YARD SALE MAMACITA
Guest starring la Chismosa

I.

The art of language is a white prom dress sprawled on the floor.

Sequins dug deep into old shag
leave you to house-wife luxuries
telenovelas, microwave home cooking and canned frijoles
when the old man lays down
3.50 an hour times sixty
you smile sweet like fifteen
reassure him with your tone
claro mi corazon es suficiente
sometimes you lie to make ends meet.

Two bags in each hand
ankles swollen like summer tics
you waddle from stop sign to stop sign
a dozen eggs, tortillas, crossword book
no one knows the young girl genius
who won the Pomona Elementary Spelling Bee *five times*
no one knows how you once wore a size six
don't you know everyone is beautiful on prom night.

II.

Aches you are too proud to let go
settle into your back like son #1
you stay buried in a Korean blanket
from a sunken sofa you zone into and out of old photos
framed and nailed to the wall
each an altar to the possibilities that haunt you
hijo querido #2 would have come home
had he never called that recruiter back
y el pendejo still calls after son #3
who sits down to do his matemáticas

cause on day he's gonna build you a bridge to paradise
made from foil, cebolla and an endless mile of sunshine.

III.

You tell Lydia, *nosy mujer*
who lives alone with twenty cats next door
that you are of Spanish descent, *una gitana*
you tell her so well, even you start to believe your own lies
a Flamenco firefly
you twirl around a 1972 vacuum
that long since choked on pennies
change best spent on visiting days too far to bus to
6 a.m. to 5 p.m.
yard sale lady
a.k.a. "mamá" "vieja" "mi mujer"
prom queen figure for sale
synched tight round the mannequin's waist
you wait for someone to be blinded by its flat light
hold your breath when it sells for thirty billetes
to la viejita loca, the one crippled in her feet
and as wide as two tires round her waist
she says she will save it for her granddaughter
la que nunca visita.

Here, where only the wind remembers you
bella... vestida de sueños sequins y juventud
she whispers lavender blessings
that make this day more bearable than most.

SUNDAY MOURNING OVER
HUEVOS RANCHEROS

another red summer burns your intestines
as you scoop sunshine with limp tortilla
from my kitchen seat I imagine the tubes that kept you alive
each a garden snake in Adam's Eden

your father stretched over the guitar
his mother left him under a broken street lamp
in Ensenada he'd play til his fingers bled
calling her to come home

at the door twin witnesses claim Jehovah is waiting
for your mother faith's a full book of matches
each votive a hungry totem
in her life there have been two kinds of men...

...those that die and those that haven't yet

I know how tight the Reaper holds you
how he buried your umbilical cord in his backyard
like a voodoo curse your carry lead in your belly
tatted prayer hands mask holes in your back

this Sunday there are fresh haircuts to get
a single file line of remaining friends
pallbearers with number in hand
waiting for the Barber to drop his scythe

VIGIL

On the corner of Figueroa & Citron
a lady sits wrapped in black lace
twenty-four candles at her feet
I should not know the number but I do.

As I pass her my speed drops to a crawl
I've fallen into a grave and she is looking down at me
her long black braid a sure rope.

I pull myself up to stand next to her
death stains my chest
glass slivers dug deep into cheeks that no longer bleed
my hands are limp salamanders
my legs rooted lichen.

Together we stare this angel down
her eyes made up with cotton candy blue
a white cotton dress
silent smile tucked away
that day she was late
her class in urban planning started at 6 p.m.
at 5:25 a mid-sized sedan took an accelerated ride
through her cross street
leaving her a mangled web of pages and skin.

For twenty-four days her mother prayed us into slow motion
her sorrow ruled that corner
her child had cities to build
violins to make sing
now parks grow from her feet
and whole blocks are cluttered landscapes of chalk outlines.

On those Saturday nights when SUVs barrel down the center lane
taking out trash cans and strays
those nights when I drive my sober ass home

wailing like a dove set free from a Jalisco jail
I see the victims of impatience lining the road
and I know it should not move this fast
this passing should catch our breath
if only for the length of a light.

HANDBALL IN LINCOLN HEIGHTS

one hundred fifty-eight roaches between my bare feet and the bathroom
twenty-one cold steps from this heap of dusty orange sheets
this must be where the police will find me
smiling like good time girls do right after they've been caught

twenty-one colds steps between my bare feet and the bathroom
at 2 a.m. Lincoln Heights needs lip gloss
why can't I smile like good time girls do right after
in these hills my cell don't work, I am disconnected

2 a.m. and a girl needs lip gloss
what do lovers in favelas do for kicks
no reception, disconnected 1st world bitch
good time girl to the nth degree

this must be what lovers in favelas do for kicks
swat palmetto bugs in makeshift handball courts
good times under cover of stained sheets, 1st world retreat
legacy of bolder women's feet worn in the tile of his abuela's floor

palmetto bug handball
must be where the last girl gave up
the sight of his abuela swatting then stomping tile floor
beady-eyed monsters retreat to the corner

standing where the last girl gave up
scared to wet myself, the sheets, abuela's tile floor
I did not come here to dance with roaches while my hillside gangster sleeps
beady-eyed monster, his legs up in the air

this must be where I come to my senses
find my shoes, pretty pink tanga, entrails of my dignity
run past abuela and out the front door
but being good time to the nth degree
I curl back into the warm body between me and my great expectations

KILLING IS WHAT HE WAS BORN TO DO

like some are born to paint
or pitch or risk their lives for some worthy cause
look miss, a poem just like you like
about real shit miss,
real like OGs get down for
his enemy's lung an impaled birthday balloon hung on the fence
red lint on white of his cap and kicks
revenge for a life of blank pages.

Being teacher I'd asked for a poem
about a memory they couldn't forget
a first kiss
a first hit from their old man
maybe their first trip to the beach
something real that they could still see
when they closed their eyes at night
like light on your corneas after the switch has been pulled down
the ardent echo of something there before.

It was an epic poem for his trigger finger
crescent moon of right thumb
pink from the squeeze
he'd made so many
their eyes like moths under streetlights
silent nods of homeboys piled in bucket seats
the ride back to the crib
where enchiladas were waiting
taste of ash and blood and beans
mud between this death and the others.

He was born to kill,
like only real thugs can
like only real teachers can comprehend
what it's like to shoot an open ended question into a storm cloud.

THANKSGIVING WITH SIN

Sin, he black eye of domino
father Blood
born on backside of industry
end of freeway 5
where Mac trucks clutter veins like clots

at midnight his mother counts alien ships
from her lawn chair
Keith Sweat serenading the block
where Sin, part devil, part man lives
under halo of urban myth

see Sin, under my skin
his kind of brown like Mississippi mud on my stretch marks
like bits of rust under my nails from swing set sessions
after strip poker and two liters of Old English

Sin, ever thankful
sets me and mamma to steamin at 4 a.m.
collards and yams
not even he will eat
turkey meat stuck in my throat
cause Sin don't date skinny girls
cause his babies sit to my right and left

today Sin both father and son
lazy-eyed martyr of a real G's life after all debts been collected
and when I want to play Bonnie to his Clyde
Sin sits up straight
tells me, *this ain't no life for a good girl*
no kind of life at all
but I know all the words to Mr. Sweat's songs
and how to season greens
how to yell domino with as much fire as ice
bet I know how to make any man happy

Sin, now father and politician
kisses my baby fat
takes me by the hand and smacks my ass on my way out
sayin, *good girl you go on home*
before you catch yourself believing you belong

JAMIE

eyes tied back with black lightening
charcoal rope braided behind her
with pomegranate lips split open, Jamie
could not say no.

While we, the restless, went fishing for richer men
she'd wait by the phone
the calls always came at 7 or 10
Lady, do you accept the collect charges?
yes, she said
yes again and again to the men we'd forgotten
yes to men we'd outgrow before their parole.

There was Juan who liked grape soda and dominoes on Sunday.
Tito who smelled like the cologne aisle in Macy's.
Bobby who never knew when to stop laughing.
Wilson with his tired one line,
"Hey baby, did you hurt yourself fallin from heaven?"
and Sweet Tyrone who could outrun the track team of the school
that asked him to leave when he wouldn't return his history book.

Jamie never said no to their speeches
their poems carved on the wall
their requests for more cigarettes more cash more letters
Jamie stayed home chasing away the high gray waves of solitary
but on some nights the waves won
and when we got home Jamie's lightening had run
down her cheeks a flood of black ink.

Guilty of abandoning our loves for good times
we'd dip our fingers in her stained sink
write of how our love would never end
that we'd wait until the Second Coming
for a second chance to hold them again
we'd promise a letter a night
until the warden had drowned in our pages.

Then the days would unwind like hot rollers
and our lips would cry out for shock red
good times would seep out from the radio and back under our skin
but Jamie she stayed on to carry our tears for us
and when I think of women most loved
by wind by storm by ink

I think of Jamie, eyes tied with black lightening
charcoal rope braided behind
her pomegranate lips on the seals of crisp envelopes
buoys for men lost at sea.

A LOVE POEM FOR A HATE CRIME VICTIM
SPREAD OVER THE MALIBU HILLS

twisted bullets thrown up into a sky too blue to hold heaven

seeds bursting with vermilion of lips yet to be kissed

eyes swollen from poison sprays melted into these mountain ranges

here, wanderers wind like rain down paths made by those who dared
        to swallow *lost* whole

let hunger worm its way through their pot bellied bodies like
        an unpolished hollow tip split into clover

clawing through sands fallen through figurine of God's time

born under mosaic arches of the Alhambra

wounded and healing in Nazi, California

hidden thirteen miles below this sea

thirteen years deep into lifelines they cut

and thirteen months later I'm still watching you bleed

Zapata brava bloodstains on orange buttercups

Your aches loiter on stones cut perfect for resting
        by sunlight and patience

can't you see your pain is nesting itself into my poetry

a lone summit on why free trade isn't really free

a hungry pipe bomb left where our unborn baby sleeps

a sickle cell on the back of a dead man's pillow

spreading still through the echo of air force jets

the hum of ancient regrets   over   bound   towards
        a mountain we too faded to climb

love enters swaying lazy like peacebreakbeat on ranchera time

slicing still through streets with names that sound plain dumb in
        Webster framed English

oh baby you do this   with your wind   your easy way

you do this and I know   if I leave   it won't be today.

BURNT
BRIDGES

Behold, how great a matter a little fire kindled.
And the tongue is a fire,
a world of iniquity:
so is the tongue among our members.

JAMES III v.5-6

BATTLE

It has been eight months
since I've looked into the toilet bowl
and seen my reflection spitting up all that is good in me
piercing my thorax with bitten nubs
blunted by years of acid reflux
index and middle worked so consistently
they now host incomplete ovals
where my identity seeped out one meal at a time.

In my locker I kept the books
no one thought it would occur to me to read.
In my house I kept score of who was winning the war,
my mother or me.
You'd think she would've noticed the cover up
water running, leftovers left on the plate
but she was busy reclaiming her body
putting on pounds he had denied her for years
it was fear that kept her bird boned and emptied.

In Psych 101 they say it is a white girl's disease
brought on by years of exposure to Vogue
sour lilies on a waif mother's vanity
a tea party of sunken skeletons
working their way through skin with gossip and tweezers
and maybe it was the white girl in me wishing her way to the front
through the layers of hip and sway
to the front where college recruiters could see her
all blonde and lean and shake her hand
without fear of contamination.

And maybe it is the white girl who is lonely now
that there are no ulcers guarding her burden
lost she wanders the mountain ranges of my body
wondering when I let go

but I know better
this battle is old habit
one like any other racist twitch
and it lives in the repetition of unloving everything we are
starving all cells equally until you become something other than yourself.

PARKING ON THE EVE OF MORE BAD NEWS

you haven't given into the forty-ounce yet
moaning when you blow on its neck just right
for tonight you make do with skin
for tonight I'm aloe vera stretched over your belly of scars

before love there are doctors
spirits and dead nerves between us
clogging pores, staining our lives like iodine
for tonight we make do with skin

though I know the dosage it takes to light the inside
I haven't given into the bottle yet
moaning when you blow on its neck just right
for tonight I take sips full of wind

if there is more to this cliff
this edge of the world romance
more than dead ends and scarred flesh
let it be found in the stars
a sacred code
charted and passed on for generations
a scroll tucked inside bottle
with news of a lost pair
in search of new skin to love with

ODE TO AN ESTRANGED LAX

Having lost my tribe,
I'd come here seeking Rosa Carmina's face in late night arrivals
someone always hugging, crying, goodbyeing
a census of parallel lives
where any rolling stone could leave at will
stretch arms, tilt hat, wave ticket and take off into the next.

I needed to know you'd never shut me out.

Now we threaten you,
must relinquish all emotion just to stand in line
with no one holding hands
everyone steaming in the ash of an unthinkable fate
pay phone receiver confirming
beyond metal detectors and unexpected frisks
in a land of dormant volcanoes
in a night of fainting blue skies
awaits one sweet melon ball kiss.

UNDER THE BRIDGE

His face a cactus paddle
arms and legs—stumps of an olive tree
the school sent a warning letter
she reads it to the mirror

behind stumps of an olive tree
the boogieman lives!
warnings left in lipstick on the bathroom mirror
she believes someone will believe

the boogieman lives,
in a manila file, under a hundred such files
she believes someone will believe
the girls in their mini-skirts, their faces made-up, shoulders bare to the sun

a hundred such files on a desk held hostage by 2nd class victims
she wipes his spit off her neck
her mini-skirt torn, mascara smeared, bruised shoulders bare to the sun
she claws her skin until there is nothing left

she wipes his spit off her neck
inside the boogieman growing
the red headed nurse holds her hand while the doctor scrapes
            until there is nothing left
under the bridge but a gym bag and broken shoe lace

inside her—an egg covered in spines
a bell rings, freeing an endless trail of 16-year-old girls
pink sweaters and pumas with fat laces
the number 2 bus with stops just after the bridge

an endless trail of girls, most walking home alone
his change swallowed by money slot
the number 2 bus with stops just after the bridge
her scars testimony, the boogie man lives.

EXIT STAGE LEFT

You, my love, are lonely
because we with spray can proverbs
have gradually made their sonnets our own
we their most aggravated wound
have taken this treasured jewel
and polished it with black soap.

You interview the dead on open mics
more secure in spotlights than séances
ask out loud where a brother can score in this town
to weather this tempest of addictions
we tour sketches of sidewalk artists
hold our ears to the wind for news of island babies
survivors of shark-infested seas
landed on jagged concrete of this New Spain.

Loving you is the first hit
lips tight round a glass river
I wonder what we'll make with the smoke and
how many turns each will take before passing?

If life has ever failed you
then know not to plant me in your heart
for I would grow there too fast
pulsing in asthmatic sensitivities
each breath a refugee from the high life
under red velvet of my sex.

My sweet unconditional, exit stage left
no song could save you from the orgy of oxtails and old habits
no summer rain could remove your ink stain from my lips.

HOUR GLASS

I. 1995

From where to where we've come and still so far from home.
I call you to be heard but you are too proud to listen.
You call me to advise but all I hear are the mad ramblings of a woman
who has turned her back on that brown baby
once stuck to her pink breasts.
This routine as much family as physics and bombs
more related than up is to down
more codependent than codeine & flu
I scream I AM through the phone, then hang myself
on the umbilical cord wrapped around her version and mine.

II. 1999

I send slides of my DNA so she can see
there is no way to avoid this life she claims I've chosen
but logic concludes with Hello
instead we discuss musicals
sing a hymn or two from *The King and I*
and for a moment there is harmony
then I remember there are Asian stereotypes
and negative feudalistic subplots to consider
I have crossed the line this time for sure
Hammerstein is choking me and Rogers is breaking through my front door
while she pounds out reasons why I am...
an unfit American, a terrible citizen, my rent late,
my car illegal, my man unemployed, my credit in ruins...
though I can't see the mess I've made
I know she is boiling over and my heart skips beats
because it knows I am no longer her little girl
and that's when we both get the point.

III. 2006
I exit a burning Los Angeles on a magic tax return check
a gallon of gasoline in one hand and pen in the other
for five months she has held in every tear
cause she is Virgo and they don't lose well
even the doctors tell me how competitive she made the last days
a race between her spit and the lymphoma
not even my rage can get me there in time
like her I refuse to cry but there is sand in my chest
in my throat building up into tumors
it takes me years to spell *I am sorry* with single grains
and just seconds for her to sweep them all away.

YOUR ISLAND

nighttime in your mother's bed is a marathon of creed
incessant chirping of coquis
abusive rain on tin rooftop
knowing you'd rather miss your island than own her

in four hours you'll call to say you're not the one
that no mystic could tap the vein to your heart

the choir only hears what they want
your drum calling Eleggua to open phlegmatic chords
hands rough from digging in other men's yards
gently tracing my pink shell
your beard's broken needles scratching
worn 45 of my laugh lines
the slow roll of a homemade cassette
your boleros holding the air hostage like you never left

BLOOD

Your boy asks where you go when you are gone
you point to a black hole only a dead man could see
there son, in-between God's eyes.

Did you think of him when you held out your arm
fist tight green veins throbbing with another punch of anthrax?
Does poison pass from father to son?

While other men saw naked angels
carved in crude oil skies
you saw healthy kidneys
two pair
one for yourself
one for your father
the man whose hands held bottles before they held yours
stumbling up rock past waterfalls and prehistoric trees
he led you up summits of el Yunque
asleep against a stump while you counted stars.

When they called your name did you know how far you'd travel
and what color you'd have to kill?
Did the blood of "sandniggahs" spill into your dreams?

High from a scorpion's kiss at night you'd see Yemaya rise
above the tanks and sleeping men
her hands cupping a turquoise sea
your son at the bottom
asleep on a bed of chicken bones.

Did you own your hate when they told you
there was nothing wrong with your body?
no toxic verve seeping from your hand to his
no pill to keep the grains of sand from filling your lungs.
At the observatory he has his own story for each light
his own reasons to survive
he has found you wounded but willing to ask for his help.

FOR THE FLOWER WOMEN

For years the family has called to tell of deaths that couldn't wait
of flower women who could no longer breathe stained air of memory
women woven of chichicaste and mud, spotted with age
alone in houses loitered by grandchildren
who still feed off sagged breasts
as steam from clay pot clings to their faces
like responsibility of having to feed one more.

The phone call is made by some cousin
who would have been brother or sister had they been closer
tired from the wake and scared to practice their English in post-mortem dialogue
we stumble together through fields of fiber optic cables
as to arrange payment of headstone, scent and color of flower,
        dress of beloved.

My father numbed by distance no longer cries
and so I ambassador to the past he's long-since entombed
navigate the river balanced on a worn cross
bobbing between one shore and the other.

It's the absence of the land that won't let me forget
her hand's ritual preparing té de canela
raised veins rubbing herbs and crèmes into my hair
the women who always had time to *pray first M'ija, always pray first.*

Now lying still, a balsa wood figurine of what I would have been
had I been born before convenience
what we the modern nameless warless childless
generation of cracked bridges are
when no one sees our heads bowed before altars we once mocked
twisted beads between bitten nails, lips tucked under with mumbled penance
feigning faith long enough to know with her dies the kind of woman
who lifts tortillas out of sand, shapes them into hearts
fills our bellies on sacrifice and with a kiss
promises tomorrow there will be more than enough.

THE ROSARY

when we make love it hangs on the bedpost
a noose stained brown by blood
a muddy river's overflow
you hold it when you drive
when we kiss your fist always between our chests
our arteries sense the history and crawl
like vines to touch salvation's erect x

on national ditch day I make us a picnic
cheezits chicharrones grapes
small plastic plates and napkins folded like cranes
a skill you say makes you believe in Pangea

instead our holiday is spent in search of the thin rope
knotted by a blind nun
one for each blip in the flatline that was your life
—you promised Him—her prayers would not go in vain
at sundown I sit on the balcony and eat without you
while you dig through my dirty underwear like Pilate's men
hunting for a trace of flesh in the shroud

ON DEFINING US

ABANDONADO, ABANDONAR, ABAJO
you were gonna teach yourself Spanish
while I was in my Don Quixote lecture
legs crossed, eyes intent on absorbing the "A" section
of my Spanish-English Dictionary
the words you choose to learn

ABANDONADO-ABANDONED, DESERTED
ABANDONAR-TO QUIT, GIVE UP
ABAJO-BELOW, DOWN

abajo tu vives
abandonado y abandono
I thought your curiosity cute
but you were not looking for a new tongue to love with
you were looking for another way to say "I quit."

HOW I LOST MY FATHER TO AMERICA*

He was there for the length of El Bigote's grito
GOOOOAAALLLLLL!
and then just like that he'd fade
into another hour-long patience
awaiting the next great angle
I'd wait with him
2,000 miles away in a sagging futon
watching a borrowed TV
that never received team *America* in full pixel form
hopeful as Cuahtemoc's granddaughter
that someday these cleated warriors would grow feathers
fly back in time to when winners were sacrificed
to when one strike of the stone ball
meant seizure or sudden death
back to when the stake's were too high
to hold my father's attention.

Without notice he stopped calling
on Sundays at 8 a.m.
and again at 9
he stopped calling on holidays, birthdays
and in-between days when he does what men do
when they have been left by their everything.

Thought it was my engagement to a communist
that left him speechless under sable palm
waiting for legitimate grandchildren to call on him to play
reason enough to try him after six months
on Sunday at 8 a.m.
and again at 9.

Listening more to El Bigote's grito
than to my innocuous good news
(como'tas papa) bien bien m'ija

y tu? (bien) okay good I love you
pray to Jesus (I pray dad, I pray)
Good (espera papá tengo noticias)
hum okay I love you Good
GOOOOAAALLLLLL!!!! (bye)

*America is the state soccer team of Guadalajara, Mexico

DON'T MESS WITH THE BULL
La Zona Rosa, Mexico, D.F.

Jesus is the cousin that makes being cousins hard
he's Infante without the mustache
a certified hottie
he is policeman and rebel
responsible and cruel
my ideal man
my adopted big brother

he forbids me to ride
the electric bull lonely and waiting
says only a puta would be so crass
so I wait for him to go to the restroom
tie my skirt high around my hips
and mount the dormant beast

this is for las adelitas! I cry
que viva la bruja, soldada, puta!
with an ay, ay, ay! thrown in for good measure
when he comes out drying his hands on his jeans
only to see me gyrating before the world
his friends making bets on how long I'll last
it's like I've wrangled his balls
he tackles
knocks me right off the bull
into the hay
into his arms

when he puts ice on my swollen ankle the next day
he swears my bruises prove him right
that there are some lessons only a man can teach

THE HOLY TRINITY AS DEPICTED IN WEST SIDE STORY

I like to live in America
Okay by me in America
Everyone free in America

I am Anita, mambo high at midnight
sweaty after a private rumble with a man I'd like to call my own
there are nights he calls for my legs only
hung over balcony like peace flags
then there are nights when I turn a blind eye to the war
only to wake my back a field of landmines & lesions
to survive you must love the fighter as much as the fight
sirens remind of a country that turns boys to assassins
no border could impede his ominous crusade
he's seen his village torched
his brother's tongue cut out
his baby aborted by the enemy's dirty blade
I am a red light salve on a wound America won't claim
but I say send me her newly-arrived vipers and thugs
I want to love them in triplicate.

America
Sweet America

I am Maria, mother of convicted killer
morning dove before God
my wings resting on oak
candles nestled in my hair
I paid for his passage with my body
exchanged his health for mine
paid for his uniform with tithes
saved from the months I was too ashamed to attend
waited up nights to see him stumble in bloody
his Sunday shirt torn
I never taught him to kill, but he learned just the same

before guns there was a mother's love
in line at the market I saw her, the other mother
she threw fruit at me and screamed, "madre del diablo"
I know who took her son and mine
it was the man who sticks needles in
prods them until there is nothing left but acid and black tongue.

America
Sweet America

I am the dress that made you look
that brought you home when you could've been out
when you could've been next
I am the satin on your skin
that asked you to dance with your finger tips not your fists
the curve and line that made you forget
for me you will pray to a God you thought had forgotten you
only he is a She and She is bombshell if you can see her
mother if you'll obey her
sister if you must devote your wars to someone's honor
at the end of night I will spin over you
dead set on delaying the last dance
a parasol of razor blades
a vow of tender flesh
a silk thread around your neck.

GOODNIGHT MOON

there was no moon the night I spent $43.50 in long distance charges
to hear you tell all the reasons I'd already heard
from my godmother my government
on why Cubans and Americans should never meet

there was no light when I left your letters
broken sacraments at the door of the only Orthodox Church
that still believes enough in God to leave its gates open at 3 a.m.

there was no silence high enough to block the celestial hum
the universal "I told you so" ringing like church bells in my hung-over heart
there was no answer no wind no you

I drew what I remembered of your face on the steamed stained glass
a map to where we left our hand prints
like an army of doves dipped in blue paint
enough to protect our nest in Trinidad
where we dared to plant wartime possibilities

your goodbye a reminder
never again will a line be open enough between us
for me to accept collect charges from your particular revolutionary star

LA BELLE BALLERINA

Like Scarlet she will not go quietly
she argues with specialists over words like "terminal" and "treatment options"
her bald head a blotchy map of resistance
the remaining hairs thin splinters of trees left after the Bomb
she pushes the nurse's hand away and promises the doctor this is not over
at home she feeds the cat, talks back to the president elect
she decides what we'll have for dinner, then too sick to join us
she retires to catch the last hour of another American Movie Classic.

In the bed where she read credits as they scrolled over her swollen womb
I catch her laughing
as technicolor lovers fight over who to invite to the ball
I take her feet in my hands
spread the tired bone and skin
massaging reminders of the nights it was her gown spinning
and the world went drunk with her grace.

TOMBSTONE INSCRIPTION FOR
A LOVER ON 115TH

When you left
I never bothered
To take the sign off your back
That read// Recovering addict
Do not disturb
W/flightless
Love things
It would only bring
Bruises//

SIZE 10
for Nehanda

exile in Havana means
your shoe collection retreats into the closet of a Harlem apartment
you once rented when times were good

in your absence we've won
arguments on identity
perched on love seats
sipping ginseng teas
flirting with affirmative action
still sprung on what it's done for us
never stretched far enough to snap back

you'd smile and say *black*
baby, that's all you got
lift your left fist to your lips
and mumble COINTELPRO

photos of your lover, Mario
remind me of JJ from Good Times
his broad-toothed smile has you open
loose like New Years 1979
but in his grip I see you twisted
a squeeze of lime into warm rum
needing love like every woman do
holding tight like every mamma do

Ms. Dalton, I see you fly past in a U-Haul truck
you took four years to find your way to that island
your baby girl crying out for a reason she could touch on
why liberation for the People meant mommy's never coming home

they say you live it
live it like a Cuban
live it like you need it
cause maybe you do
a burst of superwoman
in and out of sweaty rooms
spilling a little secret here or there
so no one forgets what you gave

you Cherí Amour are grandmother to a beautiful ward
she, like yours and the fists before
lost in choices no sane women should have to make
from fifteen stories high you yell *Happy New Year!*

I came here to shop for feet I've only seen run
two for one at Payless
cause mamma you sho'nuff lived up to your size ten

SO AND SO

when we were children
my friend Lisa, the Baptist
told us suicide meant Hell for those who dared
to slice or swallow their way out of His grace
I told her to go to Hell cause my cousin was in Heaven
right where she belonged

when we were children
Charita came to my sleepovers
braided Lisa's hair into cherry-sized knots
and sang us all Bobby Brown's prerogative
in the morning she'd go back to the Southside of town
where Africa had settled 200 years ago against its will

when we were children
Central Avenue might as well have been the equator
slicing through our bicycle routes like crime scene tape
making us as curious as we were scared to cross
over the years we'd grow into strangers
shadows of an original hate
we could not remember why
we were no longer giggles in unison
when corn popped out of kettle into our wide-opened mouths
we could no longer remember when the doors to our houses
became steel plates between the nations taking cover from each other

rumors spread round those who know
you used to know so and so
and so I heard Charita was now a dancer
pumping hard at night
by the dim lights of club Atlantis
where baseball players doubled as pimps
for dentistry students and single mothers

rumors spread round those who know
you used to know so and so
and so I heard Lisa traded in Sunday school
for keg stands and best friends
who all called her whore
when number 54 said it was her with him and number 23
behind the bleachers she'd bleed onto her white pom pom shorts

and when I heard what I heard
I didn't defend the two loose-toothed girls
I'd once told all my secrets to cause I knew
they knew what they'd heard on me too
how I was a gang-girl now
bandanna beat downs to my credit
how I lost my virginity playing spades in an alley
where runaways converged to plan the next 7-11 heist

looking back it's hollow how
we came to trade each other in on slave blocks
outbidding with rumors of masters we'd conquer
someday I'm gonna pop some corn
and send my baby to deliver it on her two-wheel ocean blue bike
to the houses where we used to sleep side by side like sisters

LAUNDRY WITHOUT YOU

bald Colombian men argue over the referees call
how they would have made that shot
these men forced to come to this country alone
sentenced by war to do their own wash
trip over my scattered load
as they reenact the goal with a crushed coke can
the mamacitas with their hair in rollers
laugh extra loud at the pile of egos on the floor

could not tell you the benefits of liquid to powder
or if beige could be teamed with the whites
soon suds consume the room
tios slip, abuelas curse, babies cry
the Filipino manager waves his cane and screams *mamatay dyablo!*
ready to slay the machine with an up-set stomach
now a three-headed monster daring us to come closer

as I bob by the donut store
an empty detergent bottle my buoy
sea foam extended from Elysian to Virgil
I note Chapter 10 in the Illiad of my life without you
is as sad as Chapters 9 and 5
the ones where I tried to wax the car and tenderize the meat
the ones where I slid off the hood down the hill
covered in garlic salt and soy

without you I have no domestic role model
no iron man chef or certified buffer
I'm missing you like San Quentin misses tits and ass
crying into fabric softeners
yeah, missing you like that, damn

TUESDAY NIGHT AT KING KING'S

for two days after I saw you
maraca clave then rum
in your hands I'd sweat lava
working my skin into blisters
I never minded
the mirrors
the ice
never asked where you were before
or where you'd go after
as long as you came

for two days after you sang
sabia que ibas a llegar
I answered each ring
expecting to hear you missed me most at lunch
midday under a bitter sun
still it was enough to dance
under your nose
with his name I've forgotten
how much I hated
hibiscus wilted behind my ear
I'd hear the rumors of your conquests and laugh up blood

pride is an island—more hell then oasis
still I missed you and you knew it
damned I went on dancing
with his name I've forgotten
the exact extent of my rage
framed by your taino afro
challenging gravity
your lips swollen with song
mocking me still
sabia que ibas a llegar

"I knew you'd come" and I did
fists first, you kissed the knuckles
then flame, you lit the candles
then spit, you filled the glasses and toasted our love

tonight the good girl is leaving early
hands full of maraca clave then rum
back steaming from the pace of the mambo
head held high this time
hibiscus coaching
don't look back
and I won't
not even when you call my name
mid-song, center stage
and that is worth the price of admission

TESTED

the pipe sighed before it gave way to the weight of the Federale's boot
long and worn it sighed the way a woman does when her man is explaining
why he must leave we were fifteen miles from the border five hours from
crossing eight from home the activist in me thought it unjust a waste of
a perfect pipe the night before cheap wine and moon Ensenada full of salt-
water puddles the licking between us the jagged line between moon and sea
they wanted me in exchange for your freedom their smiles filled with silver
their tongues forked with the thought of the trade laughing at my white girl
English (the kind I turn on when I most want to know the truth about men)
they made you do push-ups two hundred and thirty-one for each mile we'd
traveled to escape ourselves and the ending we'd promised we'd never let
happen your arms heavy with the weight of your duty to protect the sigh of
your chest under the Federale's boot a reminder that love is not the shadows
we left dancing by the fireplace but a showdown between us and the world

TESTED II

what does it matter, positive or negative
my cells have a secret to tell

what does it matter that I knew you a lifetime or one night
that a simple question could have evaded this wait

what does it matter, when in the moment precious is as she does
and she does what she wants regardless

what does it matter, this endless week at Lammle's, Borders, the page
celebrating the flutter of everyday

what does it matter, the answer
if Eve has already taken her bite of infinite sin
and being great-granddaughter there can be no hope for me

what does it matter, the answer behind that door
in a room filled with Kleenex and cushions
in case I don't take the news well

what does it matter, the nurses are on lunch, all except one
it matters to her that I know before the worry on my fingertips spreads
from one magazine to the next

and what do you care that on the way home there is only Springsteen
and that I've known every word since birth
you can't start a fire without a spark

what does it matter that he's right
or that I've survived another day
having been skipped over by the wild flames

what does it matter when the house of my neighbor will still burn

TESTED III

cacophony — the sound of a 4th grade music class

disingenuous — me the last time I took on a Puerto Rican drummer

harangue — my mother on finding out about said Puerto Rican drummer

fell — he fell my heart like a lumberjack in a sacred forest, no one heard
the crash but me

plunder — I plunder through the sales rack to work through the ache

these words borne by the mouths of men I never trusted
branded into my brain with each repetition
with each florescent flash card
closer to 600

"You must improve two hundred percent to be considered for our program,"
must twist and tame tongue to this foreign vocabulary
this multi-syllabic regime of founding fathers

it's Friday night
the kitchen staff is cleaning
their salsa beats tug at my feet
stuck in the drill of ages
proof of worth
scale of words
Oxford has swollen my tongue
tongue that would rather kiss
spout poems or talk shit
it is 10:35 p.m. and there is no end
to the droning academic klan in my head
I deny them their last words, reclaim my day
and slip away in grooves on the floor

WHY I LEFT WITHOUT SAYING GOODBYE
for Ebony

my thesis on the teachings of Ghandi was left on the Greyhound
between Cambridge and Port Authority I'd let that prayer go
cornrows half in-half out, must have scared a few
laws of nature say, a lioness cannot be arrested for protecting her young
but the warrant was written anyway

at Harvard it's illegal to leave your hot comb on the stove
to play Tupac before noon or after six it's illegal
to eat out, laugh loud, ash your cigarette on the pretty red brick
jagged and awkward as two county beds we dared to stay on
but there were too many martyrs that summer
ghost fists eager to punch holes in hallowed halls

still see you in the mirror,
can sometimes feel your hold on my thick mane
wonder where you are and who you've trusted
if you ever left the Brenton Harbor projects again
swore it was all good so why Harvard burn still
in my chest water fountains soothe the public
and thirst is still free, ivy league burn bridges
but we   we   throw   bricks

PUNCH LINE

I. Meyer Lansky – the name of the Jewish Mafioso we couldn't remember at 2 a.m.
II. Muhammed Ali – a hero we can both claim
III. brick walls – why my head always aches after leaving you

After a night of you & Jack Daniels
a dream of myself in a chapel with Meyer Lansky & Muhammed Ali
brick walls topped with elaborate paintings of Heaven & Hell
dare devil anarchists suspended in a cockleshell
pace the room to find a crack in the wall
a million questions gather behind my teeth;
like how many angels did they see at the bell?
is there an afterlife after the fall?
could I walk away with my guard down?

Subdued by the steady stream of blue river above
the sneering red river below
Muhammed Ali, Meyer Lansky and me
sit suspended on wood chairs like lions
waiting for the punch line to crack its whip
we take turns saying the show will go on.

So this is love just before the straight jacket
the sting operation before your number's called
this is the hull of my heart throbbing with afterwords.

ON THE VERGE OF THE NEXT RIOT

the monster grill of a Mac truck in your rearview could cause panic

my lover is driving for the first time since he hit a tree
and took a well-deserved nap

it soothes him to know I know the songs on 93.1,
the classic *classic* rock station

how Pink Floyd & lasers suit me fine as Prince & pink lace

we agree the children still don't need no education, what they get
from concrete is enough

*we interrupt this broadcast to bring you breaking news
on the Donovan Jackson case*

a hung jury

another black boy beat down

two white cops balls big enough to cheer from their pews as if
taken by the Holy Spirit

education is winter on his auntie's TV screen

a faded buzz of more to come

valley of smog pierced with high wired toothpicks set up to receive
cell phone soliloquies

a halo of radiation 10 miles wide

20 million microwaves and me with one weak heart

tell it on the mountain, I'm on the road—again,
with a man who can't sing but sings still

tell the black boy, hands tied behind his back, face against the police car
reason has interfered

the city burns to burn behind us, it's desire channeled
by the matches in my pocket

will the willing pay $2.50 a gallon to turn back

at the next exit I cry for the aunties on their plastic sofas, the police
"just doing their job," the long- horned trucker
bullying his way through it all

OBSERVATION NOTES FROM THE NEW WORLD ORDER

Psst!, psst, psst!
Is anyone there? Anyone listening?
Someone looking? Even a heart?

SUBCOMANDANTE MARCOS

MISSING

"...for men must work
and women must weep
and there's little to earn
and many to keep
though the harbor bar be mourning"
—Charles Kingsley

Juan Abrego misses his wife
when he steps off the metro
and just before the wind hits his back
he can feel her breath on his fingers.

He misses his country
the green mountain
the stoic trees
the neighbors and their animals
underfed and overworked he misses most
the little girl with eyes as black as his
who smiles in her sleep
the swinging hammock
the sprawling song of his father's farm
field of corn where they first made love
the child bride and groom
he held her hand and promised not to take long
the vow between them sewing together the hours.

Today Juan Abrego wrote his first paragraph in English
my wife has eyes like twin stars
he has begun to translate the loss
how you say extrañar "missing"
how you say solo "alone".
Juan misses chasing the crows off his land
the uncles gathered to watch the game
a rock he touched everyday on his way home.

But, good luck does not reach this far.
You have to return to its source
my wife has skin like honey
my daughter is a dancing sparrow
the letter is read to the class
then sent with a crisp hundred dollar bill
each with their own envelope to fill
the life they left
the lone woman sowing the field
the black eyes hiding
the child grown tall as the stalks.

IN MONTAÑITA OLD AGE IS A GIFT

for the victims of crossfire

there are days when the daughters think to sit on the porch

sip the same lemonade

a brew of what's gone sour in life

instead they stay in

hold babies tight to their chests

it's best to lie still

pretend you are dead

so when the beast comes

he can roll you over

maul your face til it's a monster's mask

leave you wounded but living

to be old as Maria & Ismenia

you must survive more changes then men

they'd been friends since the rivers ran blue

spirit twins too busy reminiscing on first loves

to notice machine guns aiming at air

how Armando made love with a flower first

sending blood to her hand her arm her shoulder

how her lips trembled

yes, it was like that with Pedro

a jewelry box after only two months

the lock carved from alabaster

shock made her drop it

the gold ring calling to her from bits of wood and shell

he never got mad once in 56 years

they laid side by side

they'd escaped the violence so many times

found refuge in fields and churches

an endless string of prayers wound around each fist

taking watch over children's children

shooting goals between trash bins

it was milk she needed

for milk she sent her grandson to the store

maybe she knew to save him

glasses shattered

sunshine turned dusty rose

their lives mixing again

two swallows

struck down by skipping stones

CHRISTMAS DINNER 1997

The martyrs of Acteal have opened our eyes ...
they left us the truth as an inheritance ...we see
how there is no justice in Mexico ... we see how arms
have come to our communities ... and are given to
assassins ... all to strengthen an army that never tires
of taking over our lands and controlling our
populations."

    –From a statement made by the
     Abejas at the year anniversary of the massacre

we sit heads bowed
praying over an obese turkey
three snow white heads
and my brown mane
grateful to our Lord
for more stuffing more meat more gravy
light and dark we sit
juxtaposed like negatives

they chatter   avoid my eyes
I am *hysterical,* liberal dead weight tied to their North Star
each a Jeopardy contestant speaking with endless expertise
on campaign finance and the *corruption* of welfare
they chew unaffected by the ten-second news flash
on another massacre below our stretched first world belt

excuse me

I search suburban streets for the remains of fifteen harpooned placentas
fifteen mothers not given a choice between their lives or their children's

excuse me

alone in a strip mall parking lot
I mumble prayers for forgiveness through the filter of my black-n-mild
as visions of reckless machine guns dance through my head

excuse me

mother, it's true
I've never mashed the molcajete with their daughters
never carried my children through jungles deep in the night
vines tearing at my face
bouquet of fear trail enough for monsters
to bound close behind for five days

it's true   I was born here
not under their piece of sky
but that does not stop their faces
from burning like champa in my corneas
their screams from bursting my ear drums

tragedy does not pause for Christ's birthday
sadness is memory
of when time began
gave birth to man
and man took his hate
shot it into his shadow's heart
saying take that   take that   take that

NEW WORLD NEWSIE

Your village in El Salvador had no school
but you made it to 2nd grade anyway,
took a mountain path past five encampments
to stand at your desk and recite the tenets of the latest leader.

Farmer Diego brought paper from the city
a peso a sheet, pounded as thin as Mayan gold.
Once you sold your boots for a book
and the captain tied you to a tree for a week.
Oh, what kind of soldier you would have made
had you stayed on to see the revolution through.

Mr. New World Newsie, can you read the trouble you sell?
Nowadays fifty cents buys a world of pain.
You stand two seconds too long, daring the red light to go green
willing business men in sedans to drive through you.

You shove Spanish news—more blood than truth—in their window
switch hands and try English—more words than art—on the windshield
headlines stain your hands and sleeves.
Can you explain why so many don't want to know?

"Good" & "Evil" went to war today. Where's the news in that?
Once you miscounted your sales and they docked you a week's pay,
still you stood at Fairfax & Adams waiting for someone to ask your name.

HORIZONTAL GEOGRAPHY LESSON

your bed is the edge of the world
where we lie
unnumbered
unhinged
tracing the outline of your United States map

you're determined to know the state capitals and their order
rainbow quilt of stoic rhombi
how free the coastal states
their furthest seams defined only by volcano and sea

my index finger trails the Rio Grande
its mud bleeding down my chest
your thumb leaves coyote tracks
guides for those that follow

this land is ours

as the politicians sleep through our rebellion
we take back California for my grandfather
Louisiana for yours
here manifest destiny dare not brand its legend
arrows pointing toward an imagined west
a muted south a lonely east a frozen north

all trains are caught still
no freeways flap close enough to wake us
this night reparations are collected in pores
opened by mutual love for a fifty-first state
free state shape of waning moon or twin bed
state with only room enough for two

AT THE JAPANESE MARKET

tangy seaweed salad
hiccups, sandals, straw mats, sweet egg
eel unraveled
longan like small investments
solitary lunchers
griddle, slurp, clanging plastic udon bowls
the endless noodle the elder will not cut
as if it were a lifeline to her mother's home in Nakasato

ground pearl crème, rice, steaming ginger tea
to trick the skin into an enduring youth
her leg kicking under the table
a nervous condition brought on by her husband's death
left foot tapping to the REM song,
this is the end of the world as we know it
a thin silver hair poking tear duct of her right eye
like salmon bone demanding attention

as a girl she was told this country was the end of the world she knew
she nodded
said nothing
what more was there to understand

mochi stuffed with red bean paste
wooden chopsticks, wasabe in a tube, pickled quail eggs
one thousand silver fish with their eyes intact
video game carjacks
a flutter in her chest
poster for a war movie peeks out from behind the sticker machine
under the bomb a fallen star pear
she squeezes, bruises it,
slides it into her purse before anyone can see

she remembers the weather man telling her today there would be sun
her umbrella knows better
eventually the noodle chases its own tail
the antsy knee will shatter when she falls
the star pear will wither into a heavy coat of loose skin
ever sweet but too worn for market

CANVAS LA

In a room occupied by carpet stains and a short white dog
we sit afflicted by colds brought on by evening runs through sprinklers
Marley's blues bob through air like soothing cough drops
as we practice minute speeches
each one of us a wind-up doll of nuclear facts
for primetime we flyer promos of guerrilla tactics
ask microwave masses to break habits of corruption
we promise there is still time to save this planet, your soul, your dog
there is still strength to stop boulder of apathy
don't let it flatten our dignity
we look deep into stigmatized eyes and say *I trust you*
to deliver your letters of intent to the doorstep of Congress
respectfully require them to uphold humanity
praise their constituents with sweet rains of democracy
tomorrow is growing in your granddaughter's belly
we know you are willing ready able
to open your wallet and make a difference.

CANVAS REDONDO BEACH

nativity on his shingle roof
World Wildlife sticker on his counterpane
Berkeley print stretched across his chest
he answers with jaded breath
what do *you* want
I qualify
I want what *you* want sir
taxes spent on life affirming initiatives
education & health care
not nuclear weapons
protection for...
You murdering bitch!
open door slammed shut
I slam right back
you sir are an extinct beast Berkeley would gladly 86
and Christ, well, he would never bless your rooftop or your front door

FROM THE BACKSIDE OF EL TEMPLO DEL XOL

Teotihuacan, Mexico

tourist don't dare wander behind this sacred prism
where eagles swoop and lizards boast crimson swallows
vendors tired of lowering labor into pesos
bow to avoid eyes of modern day Dons
their arrogance carved with flanked hearts into spine of maguey
names deep as linoleum print of conquest
now pressed into jerseys and sweats
what is left on the backside
are cement sheets painted with blood
segun los guias who use every tactic
to seduce gabacho wide eyes into big tips
above us prayers float in on drunken hummingbirds' wings
sudden and free they parry a millennium of tacit questions
but all I want to know is if we can blend into this ancient compass
make love like serpentine statues
twisted as wild flames on this shadeless day
and get away with a little conquest of our own

ON THE ROAD TO SAN CRISTOBAL
DE LAS CASAS
Chiapas, Mexico

Can you sleep with a semi-automatic in your face?
this is first class baby
reclining seats no chickens the bathroom door stays closed
Terminator I & II on the screen

Where's your passport?
the barrel fits into the canal of your neighbor's ear
four men escorted off like bleating calves
the bus driver continues on

Where's your birth certificate?
in your underwear drawer in your tia's house
in Colonia del Valle about 12 hours north
You are American?
American by birth?
And your VISA?
"I'll be back" the sergeant says and you know
he has seen the movie before

What to do with a pocha on the bus?
What to do with Guatemalans lined up alongside the road?
too many to turn back
too pocha to turn in
a ballpoint pen bribe
nail clippers and a tin of Godavi chocolate
the family will understand
it was me or the truffles
the truffles they say

say goodbye to the Danes
suspected socialists
and the German hippie with only one shoe
the bus driver takes a sip from his flask
what'd I tell ya, this is first class baby

you take a sip too
ask what else there is to watch
something to make us laugh a little

and there from his cabinet he pulls a cassette
of all that is wound right in the world
a Cantiflas video, "Romeo and Juliet"
silly love, man versus his own comic timing

our nerves melt with laughter
abuelos children surviving members of our international load
hyenas in the high mouth of this mountain god

the next stop isn't so bad
even the militia can't help but watch
from the corner of their eyes—a smile
reminder of when Mexico owned Hollywood
la Epoca Dorada, the Golden Age
when a short man with big ears and pouty lips
turned his people to the politics of survival
that is the politics of laughter
contagious as the politics of fear

WOMEN WITH WALK

para las mujeres del Isthmus de Tehuantepec

fast in stride
don't slow down for strays or splinters
earlobes stretched with swaying gypsy lanterns
baskets of jicama on their heads and tissue between breasts
should they have to pee somewhere deep in the Sierra Mixe
they don't wait for sunburnt tourists to begin the bargain race
they take what they ask for nothing less

breaking into rivers
eucalyptus strapped to their back
moon in their belly
a child on each hip
they slip into and out of this isthmus
unaccounted for by any government census

broad and strong
don't waste time on faith
they prefer stone
carved in times when what was   was
they brush their teeth with blood
paint their nails with wings of market flies
as their children steal bread from men
who haven't been home to eat in ten years

stretching our earth's crevices
balanced on torn feet
they spit back sand into sculpture
lungs full of iguana teeth
all the while outlasting famines
feminism and non-profit foundations

BASIC TRAINING

Miguelito writes *Viva Zapata* in dust collected on the van
his fist size of an over-sunned tangerine
in my Bruce Lee camouflage
he tells me I look like *watcho*
watcho?
watcho.

machine gun simulation
of government watchmen
he hides at the river
dares me to jump from a log draped in algae
double dare?
double double dare.

from here you can hear training drills
sharp turns & loading clicks
hand-in-hand
a wasp scares us into action
better to belly flop then be stung
the war paint washes off
his worried look gone young
a smile that says I've completed basic training

BASQUET

a lesson in Tzonzil math

10 fingers of red clay
spread across a midday sun
an impossible shot

14 skirts of black wool
chase and praise each other
ponytails up by one

28 arms for carrying wood and guns
wave for a chance to shoot
love passes love delivers love scores

history is boys waiting
taking their turn on sidelines
eyes fixed on the lassoed god

OLMEC HEADACHE

Jalapa, Mexico

fat face
squint nose
stuck in shadowed showrooms
just begging for a kiss
I see you Father
and I spot you
two thousand years in exchange for this...
that you might grow
Botero wide arms legs and chest
wobble through *their* cities of glass and wire mesh
dig through *their* modern graves
taking from them only the best
with which to start your own museum
now with *their* babies skulls encased
laugh us up an earthquake
and put an end to this nosy race

PALACIO DE BELLAS ARTES
Mexico, D.F.

Inside walls hiccup colors
brighter than Bubble Yum
bursting from Tonantzin's lips
her laughter bouncing off polished tile
as billfold politics call on her to scream
in a million shades of red
this new Mexico is rational!

outside street clowns billow flames
in the shape of plumeless eagles
awing atheists and taxi drivers
in between green lights
face-painted oil barons
mouth with singed lips
this new Mexico is rational

in Maria's Internet Café
arthritic commies sip tea while masked
teenage rebels mass email IMF secretaries
a virus that reads... this new Mexico is rational...
fwd: this new Mexico is rational...

en Estadio Azteca beggars in bleacher stands wave
row by row they cheer on Red Cross nurses
Chicadee boom a la bim boom bah!
Que viva este nuevo Mexico...
Rah! Rah! Rah!

at los Pinos* there are logs
covered with drumlines of devoted termites
served in tacos to children with silver teeth
each with a cleaning uniform that reads
Juan, first son of this new Mexico

                              in hallowed halls there is comedy
                              a drunken skeleton of Tin Tan
                    making love to his left palm on opera night
                              an endless flicker of florescent light
                    reveals prayer slips stuck with wads of gum
                              to the under seat of velvet chairs
                              dios mio este nuevo mexico es...

in the gift shops there are oxygen masks
and thirty-pound books on Orozco, Siquieros and Rivera
their mistresses chaperoned by robot slaves who flip the pages
an endless stock of postcards advertise
this new Mexico is rational
this new Mexico is rational
stamped and sent out on trails of volcanic smoke
inside swirling ribbons tickle marble slabs
all clean enough to eat on

                              outside the hunger for edible paint goes on
                              untamed by the good press

* *los Pinos is the presidential residence in Mexico City*

CHINESE NEW YEAR IN HAVANA

dragons dare drunks to dance on rooftops
lovers twist egg noodles on chop sticks and kiss
between bites bodies drift in with offerings of ron y rice
there is fire in some eyes
distant memories of a land not surrounded by time
long brown legs tight like husked cane
wide hips gripped by callused hands
exiled panthers, pardoned poets and madmen
thumb prints that leave no trace
history burnt off to protect them even here
they share scars and indiscretions
their children tuck fortunes into seashells
passed back-n-forth on the crests of West Indian waves

POLISH

Sancti Spiritu, Cuba

we break into earth one stab at a time
our work song *Sancti Spiritu, Sancti Spiritu*
our harmony careful
we may be sisters but we are still strangers

with the patience of a midwife the ghost of Celia Sanchez watches over us
her fingers long rays of sunshine tilling ageless universal matter

woman here have perfect nails
painted in garnet, corvette, cinnamon red
none chipped, none dirty, perfect-perfect red

all I have are nubs
bitten stumps where my womanhood would be if I'd let it grow
I show my mentor Lourdes my hands and look to where the pigs are slaughtered
she doesn't say a word
which I know from workshops
means there's nothing nice to say

below folds of earthworms are cut in half and I am torn
between letting her know how hungry I am or digging deeper
her laugh unveils my dilemma
taking off her gloves she says, "tienes algo pa'esconder"
nervous because I do have something to hide
even those in solidarity can be a danger to a nation floating outside the box

our last day together
I present her with two new shades
copper/silver—pennies/nickels
loose change planted in the soil of a country
that hasn't forgotten its promise

PORT AU PRINCE

a choir of ebony angels sang on both sides of the plank
leaving thumbprints on my temples
mosquito bites burnt into my sides

as tall as their steel drum
I swayed to its hollow call
wanting to be wielded smooth like that

children sprinted alongside the bus
climbing I wore matching yellow shorts and shirt
a giraffe on the chest and visor with straw bill

some could not stand the guilt
their dollars waving from windows
the barefoot hunger jumping like Go Fish

I did not have to give
but my mother she carried plastic grocery bags
filled with old clothes sandals tennis that no longer fit

the road to El Citadel a wound chambered nautilus
my donkey led by the boy with a gum green watch
that played Chopin's Minute waltz at every quarter hour

when he held my hand to help me down
I knew he knew I loved him
would have held his hand the whole way

but there was a bus to catch, parents watching a five star dinner waiting
a whole nation to attend to
far more hungry than my budding breasts

TRAVEL GUIDES
Verdadero, Cuba

The cock of a modern Master is only hard at dawn and dusk
for twenty minutes a day she congratulates him on his conquest
the rest of their time spent on the balcony of Hotel Paradisus.

Friends from nursing school gather to observe
their respective dates sipping pink drinks by the verandah
off-duty they practice names of body parts in Latin
there is a test next week but one sits quiet
busy with daydreams of pigs bled in her uncle's field
six short corpses drawing nothing but flies.

In the morning she lies still long enough to feel the sweat from his palm
sink into the warm cave between her thighs.
He never knew her name
did not ask her age at dinner
or when she danced for him on jagged parapet of El Morro.

She has been his docent for a week
guided him through the old and new of Havana
translated the menu, taken his pulse, lotioned his back
all to feed her family meat for the month,
buy a bicycle for her brother Leonardo,
who paints naked women on palm fronds—their silhouettes
left to dry in the sun,
and a TV for her oldest Victor
who spends his days cleaning hotel rooms
where he can catch the latest steps broadcast on MTV.

She gossips with her godsister Tita
on local men caught with their pants down
her godsister Tita who has walked this tightrope longer
and can say her alphabet in German, Dutch and Portuguese
her godsister Tita who believes revolution costs nothing
but what you are willing to sell.

GRASS

Squaw Valley, California

I. Sergio pushed the insatiable mower singing Frank Sinatra's
My Way in broken English he did not notice the white moth
caught in swinging blades or his abandoned cigarette
sparking a patch of dry matted grass
with a rubber sole meant to last him three winters he put the cherry out.

II. It took the brothers ten years and 3,500 golf courses
to save enough to bring Doña Lydia here and now that she's home
she sits staring out the window of their single room apartment
dreaming of an uncut green like the one in Lacandon.

III. When you blow on it just right you can set an Andean flute free
postcard of a time when sheep ruled and our only duty
was to play them to sleep with songs of cud and endless campo.

IV. For $5.25 a square foot you can buy a patch of evergreen shag
lady on T.V. says for 59¢ a day you can feed a starving child
I write a check for six and send a letter to my congressman
asking for an increase in home improvement taxes
enough to stretch a football field across the cracked earth of Somalia.

V. Underneath cleats, bent reeds of garden grass are sending out a call to arms
through subterranean telephone wires there is talk of a movement
to take on these overgrown larva with their driving ranges and grazing tanks
to rise up fourteen feet in a day and tame them into lesser beings.

WINDOW SHOPPING ON BROADWAY
Downtown, Los Angeles

she stares at her reflection in the window
a showgirl's figure superimposed
on her own round silhouette
her huipil is stained with red clay
black birds dance across her chest
their caws fending off men
who lean in with *mamacitas* and *bonitas*
their accents and beer steaming the glass

there is no harvest of wool here
no poppy seed dye
crushed red grasshopper
no loom between her legs
here women's feet press cold steel pedals
their sewing machines hidden
behind garage doors here women
dress their worn fingers with band-aids

at the ends of each arm
she sees the palms that once shuttled rainbows
the lines of yarn held tight to the loom
she remembers the rug underbid
by another weaver two stalls down
and her grandmother's plum-stained hands
waving to clot the bleeding sky as her bus pulled out

betrayed by their own uselessness in this new world
her hands press up against the warm glass
beyond her reflection a rack of leopard print
pants suits cut to hug a size six
calling on her to begin the day
in someone else's body

CLEAR GOLD
Imperial Desert, CA

one gallon
two lips
split by a river of endless thirst
hot flood of desert paint
washes off silt semen sweat
and when you arrive
there will be no paradise
just beef jerky
bile and an endless mile to go

a silent rock
balanced on the head of another
a look out cross warped horizon
its every layer touched by the devil's shaking finger
rippling tide of sand
and no man no woman or child
shall be forgotten

five gallons
ten split lips
the thirst of an emptied sea
ravine of shoes and shit and silence
a cactus field of winter roses
shell and somewhere
a young girl carries a water bottle to gym class
an expectant mother fills the dog's bowl
a tired waitress brings her table fifteen cups of ice
lemon margaritas on the rocks
slushies
fountain drinks
courtesy cups
an endless mile to go
twenty-six gallons
fifty-two cracked lips
split with the gush of air

an opened promise
between Rock Mountain and the Arco station on US 2
51 blue flags swarm
desert flies
awkward and bumbling in an alchemist's wind

change is uncertainty of the mind
menace of sanity melting
with each surge on the thermometer
107...108...110 points of lava
walking on hot coals
the endless mile behind you

two water towers sliced
a bloody foot stumbles
between this world and the next
a fever
a succulent plant
a sunrise on stilts
a pair of waning eyes
two cracked lips
a sip of clear gold

RIPE

City of Industry, Los Angeles, CA

sing her a song
a merengue line
a slip on glove
made of lace not plastic

marry her to the fence on Alameda and Manchester
where she stands under parasol of circus colors
cutting symmetrical wedges
coconut cucumber mango mamey

fingers red with chilé
lips a cracked slice of watermelon
tight from salt sticks dipped and sucked on
a desert survival trick

she reads the license plates of each passing car
writes them down in a code no MIT prodigy could break
it is the language of ancestors
glyphs used to transfer an entire civilization to an unknown plane

the clean-up of precious fruit takes ten light changes
two pairs passing in each direction
a steady gutter growl of Broncos and Mactrucks
exhaust of two-ton machinery clinging to her shoulders neck back

in La Ceiba she would make plans for Fridays
be dressed for Club Luna Llena by ten
a DJ and a tent wide enough to set sail for a warless country
her worries dampened with the ardor of good times

today she's too tired to plan such freedoms
the Bandamobile passes Umpa! Umpa! Umpapá!
a reckless toucan blaring
memories of her life before red lights

HE'S GOT THE WHOLE WORLD IN HIS HANDS
San Francisco, CA

black lung flip mop rock breath
swabbing the seams
you see the whole world from here
your own roof in the Mission
the man picking steak from his teeth
the trolley falling back
and Reverend Moss picking his scab in Golden Gate Park

the wind creeps under your hard hat
she whispers *war is on,*
it's an election year,
you'll never know how much they need you
good people of this city
disgusted by your squalid hands
your eternally-black nails
the smell of tar tainting their tranquil day

this morning your daughter
remembered to wash her hands
waiting outside the restroom door
you hold her backpack
cold damp of pipe water
steaming between your palms
as you walked her to class

MERIENDA
Sancti Spiritu, Cuba

women talk over scores of last night's domestic disputes
their nails spread petals of poinsettia
no car no cell phone no house
they own only their loves
wrap themselves tight in them
licking and smoothing the edges like cigar rollers in El Laguito

as we graze on green tomatoes and stale bread
they dissect the latest novela broadcast from Brazil
as they chew and chat
inhale Popular cigarettes
we pick up enough attitude to know the subject is men

city girls we click in similar tongues
how we left our men behind
to travel to school to taste other lips
they laugh, say our men are thick veins in the sides of our necks
throbbing reminders of how weak we can be

what doesn't translate is our pride
an overfed capitalist trademark
the Ego thinking it can do it all, alone
how far we are from love they say
from the surrender, we should be so lucky
to know when not to let go

UN BESO SURREALISTA PARA LAS CINCO
Y PUNTO DE LA TARDE
Madrid, España

Pedro the Cruel has left his jockstrap hanging in the window again.
Cousin Dalí is tanning hides on the rooftop
while Cirque du Soleil cast members play
olley olley oxen free in the garden maze.

North African hustlers slang mix tapes to museum docents
while I sip malt beer to chase down sardines and eggs.

On the way to see the King
I stain *la Güernica* with red lips meant to survive sex
they take me away in a cloisonné egg
to where Señor Lorca is hard at work
digging his own grave on the roadside of this new republic.

What would it be to die for your land your lover your goat?

I chip in, ask what he has planned for the afterlife
he answers, *heaven is making whoopie in the cobalt sands of Atlantis.*
drunk with port stolen from the liquor cabinet of the Queen
we brave the sea, only to drown just out of reach of Asmodea's rock.

CHRISTMAS SHOPPING IN MADRID

slick black leather   strapped to the backs

     of brujas   from Goyas' final days

dark as a moth eyes   they smoke chains around their lungs and mine

timing my move   I dare   to break   their shopping routine

each sucked in face   an excuse   not to give me directions

so who told Columbus   which way   how did the boy

ever find the palace   with all this pushing

and shoving   for gold   did he wander   for days

choking on the people's lack of concern   no wonder

         the man would land so lost

PISCINA PACIFICA

PELIGRO!
NO SWIMMING!
still the three-year-old china poblana goes in
to hide from the water monster
her father, un pelon con seaweed locks
tattooed from his neck to his ankles
with a map of forgotten urban planning districts

a few waves away, surfers, really accounting execs
meditate on spiked hair of Lady Pacific
I have seen her swallow three strong men on a day like this in Manzunte
their boards spit out like toothpicks
from here She's just another calculating club trick
reeling in cholos and cotton swabs alike
her hunger does not differentiate
bones boards bravado
it all goes down the same

oil derricks to my left accent the shit refinery to my right
my mother's voice says it's crude to call it what you want
it's still paradise's bidet
PELIGRO!
my big toe split by a Bud bottle, half full
I want to know why there are dead ladybugs in the sand?
Do islands have feet that tickle the sea floor?
And if high tide is ever ashamed of her lows?

CHILD OF QUESTIONS

"Live your questions now, and perhaps even
without knowing it, you will live along some
distant day into your answers."
—Rainer Maria Rilke

in between the underwear ads and the text of the presidential address
there is the question only a child would dare ask   *why*
in 1941 it cost 5 cents to print the compound equation of all our doubts
six generations later there are still no answers

we appear cleaner than we did yesterday
our hands tied to the remote
we watch shrapnel burrow in an endless desert
an engineering student seared *live!*
the school of mud walls collapses *live!*
a maidservant's lung perched on bayonet *live!*
our perverse uncle burnt in effigy *all live!*

child of questions sing sweet reason
make of your eyes reflecting pools
catch them at their windows
stop them mid-sentence
barking into red phones
their tongues barbed with this nonsensical language
its rules always bending to make way for exclusion
child of questions fight off your ABCs
block print apathy A B U
Abu Haider is taping his windows
he will stand alone to defend his bookstore
his daughter's questions ringing in his head

fifth graders down the hall spin 50 Cent
cause they gonna get rich or die trying
the war drum is bouncing down Hoover in a 67' Impala
red and white stripes whipping from the chrome rims
child of questions driving uninsured
his sagging-jean resolve to get back at The Man
a wardrobe not afforded peace of mind
the terminal *why* scraping cement

TWIN TOWERS

Downtown, Los Angeles

At first glance you look
streamlined conveniences;

like any other office building
mauve wall, vending machines,
manicured trees

you make it seem easy to enter
and then at the red light
wondering how
could enjoy
slight tease of window

friendly for visitors
stray eyes stare too long
any business man or woman
a room with no view
a diabetes test strip

if we were to prick your walls
open your slants enough

with seismic pins
to let light in

how many stones would fall loose?

how many elephants would
charge through?

ODE FOR THE MIC

for The World Stage, Leimert Park, LA

through time you stand a shepherd's staff
herding profits and derelicts
heroes too
souls intent to do right by the world
under red light
spit in your pores
an obelisk dipped in honey
you stand to make love
like stela in Copan
resurrecting history with each voice

I've seen men catch seizures after just one dance
hurling through their concrete façade
I've seen you make them cry
still they come back
with whooping cough confessionals
in solemn whispers
in eloquent rage
the pay off is hearing their name called

you are Pied Piper's flute
Trinity's anchor
Moari spear
Jacobin's bayonet
San Andreas faultline trembling
Liberty's backbone aching
thermometer rising
bass string pulled tight
playing the scales of our breathing
our over-heating
our melancholy brand of new world jazz
an antenna calling all channels home
and when the city burns again
you'll prove descendant of Black Eye Brahma
digging center to where sanctuary waits

and when the bombs drop too close
you'll turn pole vault
lifting us over and out of despair

and when they finally discover the dissidents
planning revolt in your lair
you'll turn Katana blade

til death you'll stand
and should that day come
we, the poets, will have our own Iwojima
raise you from the soft skin of death
to your rightful post center stage   all eyes on you

THE DAY I HUGGED SONIA

for Sonia Sanchez

a thousand bobby pins
jumped from the island virgin's hair
as she read of white petals and cosmic touch
heart to lung
a chorus of katydids sung
with Sonia suddenly the Muse seemed noble and fair

the day I hugged Sonia
the streets of South Central held an impromptu parade
in her honor children spun ribbons around streetlights
maypoles and madrigals
there was dizzy joy
bubbling up from the shanties of Santo Domingo
and in Quahiniqualapa black was beautiful again

the day I hugged Sonia
atheists took to forgotten maps in the stars
only to find their families waiting
at Union Station beggars were anointed
with Frankensence and Myrrh
the Earth shook along its laugh lines
and the pen in the hand of the White House
could not hold still long enough to sign off on war

the day I hugged Sonia
a monsoon of good will struck my right cheek
and being reborn I could not fight back
a window opened in my chest
a feverish pot of rice and peas thrown out
a desperate need to feed the world
to scratch and pull at the scalp of freedom
until it tingled with possibilities
and it would be naïve to think
she felt such things in my humble embrace
but she would have had to been blind

to not see the smile on God's face
when Sadako's paper cranes turned flesh and feather
lifting cataracts of smog from the pupils of our estranged cities
able to see for the first time
people gathered in parking lots to dance under an ultramarine sky

the day I hugged Sonia
a life time of poetry didn't seem so long
didn't seem long enough

INDIA

for the children of Shaw, NE, D.C.

you were seven
the world ancient
everyday you took the globe home in your backpack
as if it were a basketball or bundt cake
you took it out to show others
this is where we are — right here
that spot is home

the day the tanks came to 6th & S
you wanted to welcome the men on duty
"they're here to help," you said and took them sweet bread
while we, the grown folk, stood behind the gates of fear and contempt
they smiled at you, dropped their aim to the floor
you took out the globe
showed them the spot
you told them they were home
and for that moment they were

that summer our block was red, white and blue
with blood and flood lights
police cars and sergeants
the war was fought while we ducked under tables
16 deaths under the age of 21
you made cards for the mothers
with a picture of the world and a star
lingering above the words "this is home"

I knew then you were not of this Earth
still I clung to your geography
you made it seem the world wasn't so heavy
and with enough sugar you could change
the aim and intentions of men
you were seven
the war ancient
still you carried us all
in your backpack they found crumbs and a compass
directions home should we be lost without you

IN THE MASTER'S YARD
October 16, 1995

We hang like voodoo dolls above the masses
only today there are no nooses
it is before Islam is a flaming pitch fork in Grant Wood's hand
before we land on Mars
before even dust.

Maya Angelou is rising from pulpit
a floating soulful Buddha
first lady of healing
her minister of music, Stevie, can't see the masses
but he knows them by the smell of sandalwood and sweat
one man for each hair standing on his back

today the scars of the whip
heal with balm of brotherly love
oils and incense burn
today, you say "Al salaam a'alaykum"
like you've been saying it all your life
like you mean it
cause you do

from the trees we descend
mixed hued girls with no roots
there's no one to tell us to go home
and if they did we wouldn't know which way to run
lost in a mist of vendors
marking the date with commerative plates and pens
tomorrow the news will say 50,000
but proof is in your pictures
shots of rolling waves
under a perfect mesh of cloud and light
framing a million promises made this day

man to man
man to woman
man to mirror
it is before you become mother to an endangered species

before my godson will learn the burden and blessing of his brown skin
before hunters have had their fun with him
Mr. Farrakhan approaches the mic with his swagger step
and though no man is perfect
you can see if the possibility exists it is here
in the smile of the son on his father's shoulders
listening as if his life depended on it
cause maybe it does

it is before I throw your bad choices in your face
and you say, my problem is I thin my poems
make me immune to my own vices
like the drug dealer I've imported from back home
who has cone to be made "man" among men
he looks lost, bronze faced with sun-bleached dreads
Malcolm T-shirt on and Africa medallion
Unity bandanna and cowry shell ring
he has converted
he is sorry
and tonight will bed down
with no thought to the clients
feigning for him to come home

forgiveness is a prayer mat at the Capitol exit
an underground railroad
and all are free to get off
stroll past Master's house
picnic on his front lawn
Salat and sunset
lawyer, mailman, preacher, beggar
of humanity let them say this
there was a day when hate was chased from the Hill
fearing the free would riot and tear the hallowed halls down
and when there was only prayer and hope to accuse them of
the masses stood guilty of believing change would come

BOTTOM OF THE NINTH

There are no pedestrian crossing signs in Tikrit

red eye target running so low

Lt. Gomez shot

and if war were turned inside out

if it was your life or theirs wouldn't you have done the same

                                        a boy running

                                        towards home

towards goat herd

a tin roof haven

a good man would have aimed lower

soldier, today you are God

let no child be left behind

the few. the proud. the brave.

dressing wounds

cameraman watching

12 billion eyes are on you

Lt. Gomez shot to protect his patrol

and if it was your life or theirs wouldn't you have done the same

(this material may not be suitable for children under the age of 12)

still, the eyes of the world can not look away

a 40 inch flat screen at the Burbank airport

suits sip Stoli, Heineken draft

diet Pepsi and pizza lodged in their molars

"Put the Dodger game on!"

today Lima is God

a shutout

the boy stuck between bases and a small tin haven

a field of goats

child with one run to go

his father's walls face west   he did not see his son fall

the sand in Lt. Gomez' socks

a pillar of regret on the chopper floor

Lt. Gomez declined to speak to the cameras

bottom of the ninth

all bases loaded

Lt. Gomez cradles the boys head

a last breath

a last hit   a foul ball

but who's keeping score

"I learned about life
from life itself,
love I learned in a single kiss
and could teach no one anything
except that I have lived
with something in common among men,
when fighting with them,
when saying all their say in my song."
From "Ode to the book"
Pablo Neruda